# THE BIG FIX

# THE BIG FIX

*How the Pharmaceutical Industry
Rips Off American Consumers*

KATHARINE GREIDER

**PublicAffairs**  New York

*Book design and composition by Mark McGarry*
*Set in Mendoza*

Library of Congress Cataloging-in-Publication Data
Greider, Katharine.
The big fix: how the pharmaceutical industry rips off American
consumers/by Katharine Greider.—1st ed.
p. cm.  Includes index.
ISBN 1-58648-185-1 (pbk.)
1. Drugs—Prices—United States. 2. Prescription pricing—United States.
3. Price fixing—United States. 4. Pharmaceutical industry—Corrupt
practices—United States.  I. Title.
HD9666.4.G742003    338.4'36151'0973—dc21    2002037023

10 9 8 7 6 5 4 3 2

*For David*

# [contents]

RESEARCHERS studying the moral development of children sometimes ask them to consider a hypothetical proposition known as the Heinz dilemma. It goes like this: Heinz's wife is very sick. If she doesn't get a certain medicine, she's sure to die. The trouble is, the medicine's so costly Heinz can't possibly afford it. Should he steal the medicine to save his wife?

In recent years especially, this dilemma has escaped the confines of the psych lab and has landed in the living rooms of countless ordinary Americans. As month after month seniors and younger working people across the country anxiously go over their budgets and wonder how they'll beg, borrow, or steal enough to pay for their medicines, they're undergoing a moral education of their own. Ever more insistently, they're asking new questions: What gives these drug companies the right to charge so much? And just what are we getting for our money?

Drug companies make something we want and need: medicines that promise to protect us from pain and illness, that safeguard our ability to keep our routines at work and at home. The pharmaceutical industry can claim for its products seemingly magical benefits, from making us look better to literally saving our lives. Behind these magical claims lies a complex product whose merits are not easily evaluated by scientists, much less consumers. Even the most alert consumers are not equipped with the necessary information or power to decide what medicine they'll take and at what price, but must rely on layers of expert middlemen—from the U.S. Food and Drug Administration (FDA), which approves drugs for marketing; to the insurance organizations that pay for medicines; to the physician who alone has the power to order a drug. All this puts the drug industry in a unique position to exploit its customers with high prices and seductive marketing. And that, in the absence of government actions to curtail their activities, is just what they're doing.

Meet the McCuddys of Ohio. Five years ago Melva Mc-Cuddy, seventy-seven, didn't need much medicine: an aspirin before bed to protect her heart. Then in late 1999, she learned she had breast cancer, and her health problems—and drug bills—mushroomed. She was diagnosed with type 2 diabetes. She had two angioplasties and, ultimately, a mastectomy. Not only was she reeling from the trauma of losing her health, but suddenly she had to come up with more than $500 a month to buy medicines, including tamoxifen to prevent recurrence of the breast cancer, the diabetes drug Glucophage XR, the calcium channel-blocker Norvasc for blood pressure, and an antidepressant to help her cope with "this whole mess," which was soon compounded by the death of her mother.

Melva manages. Although she has no insurance coverage for prescriptions, a modest pension from her late husband William's job as a newspaper photographer supplements social security, and she takes a bus to Canada, where prescription drugs are much cheaper. But she is upset. She worked, supervising university field research, into her seventies—even took freelance jobs while she was home raising three kids—and William worked steadily from the time he returned from his post as an aerial photographer in World War II. "It just kills me," she says. "For those of us who went through the depression, through the wars . . . well it goes through your mind that you have worked all your life for the profits of the pharmaceutical companies."

Get Melva on the subject of prescription drug costs, and before long she's liable to mention her son: She worries about him. A self-employed realtor, Jim McCuddy, fifty, had a severe heart attack two years ago and endures a host of related chronic conditions, including worsening asthma and depression, that have him on a dozen prescription medications; some are pricey new bestsellers. Jim recently discovered his insurance premiums were going up to almost $700 a month; he just doesn't have the money, so he has dropped his prescription coverage. And what about the $900 monthly cost of his medicines? "I can't pay it," he says gloomily. "Luckily my doctor has been helping me out with some samples, but if those run out I don't know what I'm going to do. I guess I'll have to talk to him about getting rid of some of my prescriptions. Hopefully it won't kill me."

And like his mom, Jim worries about his own son, twenty-eight-year-old James W. McCuddy; last winter he started vomiting blood—an ulcer. His two brand-name prescription drugs cost about $200 a month. That may not seem like a lot. But Jimmy works as a cook for $8 an hour, with no benefits. "It takes a week's check to buy his prescriptions," says his father.

The McCuddys' struggle to pay for medicine—and that of the millions who share their predicament—could hardly fail to win our sympathy. But making drugs is expensive, right? Well, yes and no. A recent study of six representative drug-makers' financial reports found they spent only 43 percent of revenues to research, develop, and manufacture their products. A very hefty slice of the McCuddys' pharmaceutical dollar comes right back at them in the form of promotional campaigns that relentlessly push the newest, hottest, and most expensive drugs, be they lifesavers or duds. Meanwhile, some pharmaceutical giants have resorted to unethical (or outright illegal) tactics to extend patents on their top sellers, cutting off competition from low-cost generics the McCuddys might be better able to afford. And while the industry's trade group casts it as a patient advocate working to eradicate disease and defend the public's right to "access" drugs, the ferocity of its lobbyists is largely dedicated to defending drugmakers' right to charge whatever they please in the most lucrative drug market in the world. Melva is right on the money when she talks about profits: The drug industry is the most profitable of any in America and has been at or near the top for a generation.

But this is about more than just prices and profits. In pursuit of the latter—a natural and potentially productive pursuit for any industry—drugmakers have become deeply enmeshed in the process that determines which drugs Americans use, and when, and why, and how we use them. As the principal funders of drug research, pharmaceutical companies today enjoy an unprecedented level of control over what we learn about their products; they formulate the research questions according to their needs, and they supply the answers. Visiting drug salesmen are often a doctor's main source of information about new medicines. Drug companies also sponsor (and sometimes design) many of the classes physicians take to continue their licenses. In some specialties, nearly every influential expert has financial ties to the drugmakers that dominate their field. Over the last five years, the industry has also demonstrated its mastery in consumer advertising, enlisting in its sales push our own vanities, hopes, fears, and doubts. In the process of broadening their markets, drug companies sponsor "disease awareness" campaigns through patient advocacy groups and celebrity spokespeople, influencing how we define illness and where we look for relief. Through so-called user fees, the drug industry even pays the salaries of FDA staff who approve or reject their applications for new drugs.

Whatever a drug company does—whether a drug trial lasting years or a thirty-second TV spot—it does to make money. Why else? In this respect it is no different from the sellers of soda pop or soap flakes. But drugs aren't soap flakes; here, it's not just our economic interests at stake but the integrity of our health system, and, ultimately, our health itself. To justify its practices in everything from pricing to marketing, the industry's spokespeople put across the self-serving notion that what's good for the drug business is good for the public health—is good for the McCuddys. They would have us believe that the industry research is designed not primarily to develop lucrative products and position them advantageously in the marketplace, but to save lives. Its exhaustive sales pitch is really "education." With drugs becoming a more expensive and, indeed, a more important tool in preventing and treating disease, can we afford to let these assertions go unchallenged?

It may be that given our faith in the twin forces of technology and an unfettered marketplace, Americans are particularly susceptible to the drug industry's reasoning. Whatever the case, the industry's excesses are an American problem that is reaching critical proportions. Among the wealthy nations that support the global pharmaceutical industry, the United States is by far the most permissive in its regulatory scheme. As other countries move to control prices and sharply limit advertising, the industry increasingly turns to American consumers for its profits. Meanwhile, America is facing a harsh economic downturn that makes it less fit to bear this burden. State and federal budgets are no longer so ample, making for bitter debates about how to control drug costs in government programs like Medicaid and Medicare. People are losing their jobs and insurance benefits. Like Jim McCuddy, they're suddenly feeling the pain of two decades of price escalation.

What they may not understand is that they're also suffering the consequences of a voracious and unsustainable business model. Over the last couple of decades, the pharmaceutical industry has consolidated dramatically and has garnered a larger and larger share of its profits from a relatively small number of new, high-margin "blockbuster" products. To create the outsized sales figures characteristic of a blockbuster, a drug typically has to be sold at a high price, for "chronic" or long-term use, to a vast number of people. This can rarely be achieved without very intensive promotional efforts. But blockbusters are not immortal; indeed, the bigger the blockbuster, the more revenue disappears when the drug loses patent protection or sustains some other killing blow—say, a serious and unexpected side effect emerges. Meanwhile, the larger the company, the more excess sales dollars it has to produce each year to meet investors' demand for steep and steady earnings growth. Just to keep up, the big players must generate a steady stream of new blockbusters—new drugs that can be sold at high enough prices and to large enough swaths of population to bring in billions in annual sales. The trouble is, this is a requirement of the drug industry, not of public health. Company X's new allergy medicine may not justify that American consumers be parted from billions of their hard-earned dollars—a situation that in many cases only stimulates a redoubling of Company X's marketing efforts. And so the cycle, which lately has taken on a frenzied air, begins anew.

This book attempts to bring together facts that have been exposed again and again by consumer groups, newspaper reporters, and concerned physicians, issues that have been debated on Capitol Hill since before color TV. It draws on a voluminous record as well as interviews with people who spend their days and years close to the issues at hand. We might think of the drug industry's territory as a broad swath of land covered by dense thickets. Here is the science of pharmacology; over there, the arcana of patent law. On one hand are the complex workings of the federal government; on the other, the quicksilver messages of Madison Avenue.

The field of medical research is the purview of one group of experts, quite separate from the economics of pricing. The drug industry relies on the expectation that few nonexperts who venture into these intricacies will find their footing. But ordinary Americans can navigate this landscape and emerge with confidence. Although some of the facts may seem obscure, the big picture—the utter folly of allowing a profit-driven industry to name its price, while quietly making over our public-health agenda in its own image—is hidden in broad daylight.

# THE BIG FIX

# chapter 1

# THE SPEND TREND

THE AMOUNT we spend each year for prescription drugs is rising, and it is rising dramatically—by some 15 percent a year for the last several years. That's about twice the rate of increase in overall health spending and five times the rate of inflation. Spending on prescription drugs has been accelerating since 1993, and expert observers see no end in sight. The federal agency that administers Medicare and Medicaid has projected increases in drug spending between 10 and 14 percent a year through 2011, with the slightly lower rates attributed to insurers' efforts to switch patients to low-cost generics and to an expected decline in disposable income. In other words, we just won't be able to afford such high levels of drug spending anymore.

Older Americans like Melva McCuddy, who tend to use more medicine, often depend on fixed incomes that can't possibly keep up with the spiraling prices. Nearly one-third of Medicare beneficiaries have no insurance for prescriptions. But what often gets lost in the debate is that millions of younger people—like Melva's son and grandson—are also suffering because of the cost of drugs. Of those outside the Medicare program, roughly 40 million, about 17 percent, have no health insurance at all, and many more have no coverage or only limited coverage for drugs.

People with insurance may feel insulated from runaway drug costs, but with insurers and employers feeling the sting, they won't remain so for long. In written testimony before a congressional subcommittee in autumn 2002, the industry group Coalition for a Competitive Pharmaceutical Marketplace complained of unsustainable increases in drug costs that not only pressure businesses to reduce employee benefits but undermine their ability to compete. General Motors, the largest private provider of health-care coverage in America, has seen its pharmaceuticals bill swell by 15 to 20 percent a year, in spite of management efforts to steer patients to the most cost-effective options. Equipment manufacturer Caterpillar Inc. has seen 17–25 percent increases in drug spending over the past five years.

Inevitably, employers and health plans will seek to shift some of these costs to workers. Health insurance premiums have started to climb, rising sharply in 2000 (by 8 percent) and 2001 (12.5 percent). In a recent survey by the Henry J. Kaiser Family Foundation, one-third of all companies reported they were likely to raise employee costs for prescription drugs in 2003. Meanwhile, many "payers" are redesigning drug benefits in an attempt to stanch the bleeding. "HMOs are dropping or scaling back their drug coverage for Medicare beneficiaries who sign up," says Alan Sager, Ph.D., a professor of health services at Boston University School of Public Health and director of its Health Reform

Program. "Corporations are cutting back on retiree health plans in direct response to higher drug prices. And HMOs for working people and their families have increased co-payments and created new tiers for drug benefits." A common example of the latter is the three-tiered system in which you pay, say, $10 for a generic, $15 for a preferred brand-name drug, and $25 or more for a brand-name drug that's not in the plan's formulary. The use of three-tiered systems has nearly doubled since 2000, now covering 57 percent of workers in employer-sponsored health plans, according to a Kaiser Family Foundation survey. Insurers in a few markets are experimenting with a new approach that lets consumers in on just how much of a premium is paid for the most expensive new brand-name drugs: Instead of paying a flat fee, patients pay a percentage of the drug's actual price, for example, 10 percent for a generic, 30 percent for a preferred brand, and half the cost of an expensive "nonpreferred" brand.

This means that after years of enjoying the managed-care trend toward lower out-of-pocket costs, insured people, like the uninsured, can expect to begin laying down more greenbacks at the drugstore. "It's a powerful trend," says Steven Findlay, MPH, of the National Institute for Health Care Management (NIHCM), a health policy and research organization.

Why are we spending so much? For starters, more people are taking more medicine. In 1992, 1.9 billion prescriptions were filled in the United States. A decade later, the annual number of prescriptions has climbed to well over 3 billion.

There are many reasons for this spectacular boom in prescription drug taking. Some chronic diseases like asthma and diabetes are themselves becoming more prevalent, leading to more drug treatment. The population is aging, and older people tend to take more medicine. Coverage for prescriptions under managed care has made drugs readily available to more people than ever before, inoculating them against sticker shock. At the same time, there has been a general shift in medicine from surgical approaches to drug therapy, partly because new medicines have been discovered to treat various chronic conditions. "We didn't have anything for AIDS fifteen years ago and now we have a number of drugs and they're expensive and people use them," says Stephen Schondelmeyer, Ph.D., who studies the economics of the pharmaceutical industry at the PRIME Institute of the University of Minnesota. "A decade ago we didn't worry about a person's cholesterol. Now we have Zocor, Mevacor, Lipitor—there are four or five drugs that are used by a very large proportion of the population for years."

Not surprisingly, the drug industry thinks using its products is a good idea, the more the better. In April 2002, Alan F. Holmer, president of the industry's trade group Pharmaceutical Research and Manufacturers of America (PhRMA) told members of the Commonwealth Club in San Francisco that Americans should be spending more, not less, on prescription drugs. Because they prevent hospitalizations and the like, drugs are "the best value in health care," the industry claims. To quote the popular phrase, the message is: It's all good. In the face of such generalizations, and given the complexity of evaluating drugs, patients buying medicine are rather easily prevented from acting like consumers of other goods, that is, from picking and choosing among products based on their quality and value. Still it's possible to parse the issue a bit more closely.

The increase in prescriptions, and in spending, is largely attributable to the rapid market penetration of a small number of new, expensive bestsellers. Consider the observations of a recent study by NIHCM: For the fifty drugs that contributed most to the increase in drug spending between 2000 and 2001, there was an impressive swell in prescriptions—31.7 percent more scripts in a single year. The increase in prescriptions that year for the 9,482 other drugs on the market was a very modest 1.1 percent. Vast new outlays for only twenty-seven drugs were responsible for about half the nation's increased drug spending. What we're getting for those twenty-seven drugs is a mixed bag. For example, many doctors are excited about the potential of relatively new (and costly) cholesterol-lowering drugs to prevent heart disease in lots of people.

On the other hand, there are cases like AstraZeneca PLC's acid-reflux drug Nexium. It stormed onto the market in 2001, ranking number six on the list of contributors to overall sales growth compared with the previous year. And yet many experts have pointed out that Nexium is a chemical derivative of Prilosec, the crown jewel in AstraZeneca's empire, and that its clinical benefits over the older acid-reflux drug are vanishingly small. Once the best-selling prescription drug in America, Prilosec's patent was set to expire October 2001, opening the way for a more affordable generic equivalent. "They've switched all their advertising from 'the purple pill' to 'the purple pill with the three gold bands on it,' and the gold does cost you," quips Schondelmeyer. This rather cynical strategy aims to get patients taking the newly patented Nexium—"today's purple pill," the company calls it—for which there will be no generic available. What's more, with promotions that feature hordes of people and refer ominously to "heal[ing] the damage" associated with heartburn, AstraZeneca may have persuaded more people they need these purple pills than really do. The damage in question, says one physician and former drug industry executive, "is related to a particularly severe form of acid reflux in which you get ulcers in the esophagus. There aren't many people who get severe erosive esophagitis. Practically everybody gets heartburn, and these drugs do help heartburn, but usually a couple of Tums will do the same thing." Thirty Nexium capsules cost more than $100. A bottle of Tums, purchased over the counter, will only set you back a few bucks.

This brings us to the issue of price. Not only are more prescriptions being written each year, but those prescriptions are costing us a lot more. The amount you pay for a prescription has been climbing steadily over the past decade. A brand-name prescription in 1990 cost on average about $27. By decade's end, the average price tag on a brand-name was $65. This is partly due to price hikes that outpace general inflation, but a big part of the picture is the continuing shift from older medicines to new ones, which tend to be introduced at very high prices and marketed heavily. One study looking at pharmaceutical costs by a benefits manager that covers 1.6 million people found that drugs available before 1995 cost on average $1 a day, whereas those coming on tap during 1999 cost $2.72 per day. As patients start taking these new and pricey drugs, drug bills naturally go up. For example, prescribing for the newer oral diabetes medicines Actos and Avandia shot up between 2000 and 2001, by 62 and 41 percent, respectively. These drugs cost double the average for the category. Thus, increased use of the two medicines helped boost the average price of a prescription to treat diabetes from $54 to $62, a 15-percent increase in a single year. Spending on oral antihistamines surged by 612 percent between 1993 and 1998, as prescribing rose, and as drugs like Claritin, Zyrtec, and Allegra—which were among the most heavily advertised medicines—edged out less expensive products. Perversely, it seems the more a drug sells, the more the drug companies charge for it: According to NIHCM, the fifty best-selling drugs in 2001 cost on average $72 per prescription, versus about $40 for the 9,000-plus also-rans.

When a new medicine is a real boon to patients, as some assuredly are, high prices can keep it maddeningly beyond the reach of those who need it most. Todd Pelletier, thirty-four, of Maine, has been taking medication for epilepsy since he was a toddler. Two years ago, he switched to a new medicine that's been much more effective at controlling his seizures. "It works better, but it's a lot more expensive," says Pelletier. He works as a bookkeeper for a hotel, and there have been times when he wasn't getting enough hours to pay the $237 monthly cost of his medicine. He would apply to a local program for an emergency supply—or put off filling his prescription. "It was to the point where it was go without medicine or starve," says Pelletier. "And if I skip a dose, well, 95 percent of the time I'll have a seizure."

## DIFFERENT PRICES FOR DIFFERENT FOLKS

What'll a thirty-day supply of Zocor or Clarinex or Celebrex run you? That all depends on who's buying. It is a defining feature of the drug industry that there *is* no set price for its products. What the customer pays varies widely by insurance status and other factors in a pricing structure that is so byzantine as to astound and befuddle the uninitiated. "It's like going into a bazaar where they say it's $10, but you go, 'Five! I'll give you five!'" says NIHCM's Findlay.

First, there's the "average wholesale price" or AWP, sometimes referred to by insiders as "ain't what's paid." Akin to a sticker price put out by the drugmakers, it bears little resemblance to actual prices and everyone knows it. That's because big buyers—players the drug industry needs to do business with—leverage their power in the marketplace to get better prices. State Medicaid programs get rebates that, by law, must bring Medicaid prices down to the "best price" manufacturers give other buyers. Then there's the federal supply schedule, which pegs prices for the federal Department of Defense, Veterans Administration, Public Health Service, and Coast Guard and is designed to ensure that the feds buy medicine at prices at least as low as those charged to the drug companies' "most-favored" private customers. Some HMOs and hospitals cut deals for drugs they buy directly from manufacturers. And finally, insurers and pharmacy benefits managers (PBMs)—the for-profit companies hired by insurers and large employers to administer drug benefits—negotiate with manufacturers for discounts and rebates, often in exchange for giving the drug in question preferred status in their formularies.

The traditional argument for what economists call "price discrimination" is that charging different buyers based on their "price sensitivity"—the extent to which high prices will turn them away—promotes efficiency. Doctors calculate bills according to a sliding scale so that they can make a good living, while still serving low-income patients. Seniors get a break at the movies because without such a discount, they'd stay home. But price discrimination in pharmaceuticals reverses the market's orderly logic. The person who pays the most for a prescription drug is the one least able to pay, the uninsured American. People like the McCuddys, at the bottom of the distribution chain, have no big player to broker a deal for them and must go it alone. Indeed, this fragmented marketplace for drugs creates a sort of zero-sum game among groups of buyers who might otherwise share common goals. For example, in 1990 Congress, intent on sending the industry a message to rein in price increases, launched the requirement to charge Medicaid the "best price." But the industry responded by raising the "best price," that is, by reducing the discounts it had conceded to private buyers. Similarly, several big drugmakers recently threatened to discontinue discount cards for low-income seniors, fearing the law would require them to extend those same discounts to the federal government's health-care program for the poor. More generally, because discounts are negotiated from the list price, there's a perverse incentive to keep that price—the McCuddys' price—in nosebleed territory.

According to one estimate, the very same drug that costs the so-called cash-paying customer $100 dollars costs the federal government $58 and goes to private insurers and PBMs for $70 to $95. But the truth is, it's hard to tell exactly what everyone's paying. Why? Because, incredibly, it's a *secret*. What is the actual price wholesalers pay for medicines? Sorry, that's a secret. Proprietary information, the industry insists. And exactly what kind of price breaks and rebates are negotiated by the PBMs who administer benefits for 200 million people? Trade secret. In other words, what's paid for any given drug most of the time is entirely beyond public scrutiny.

"How can a market work," asks Schondelmeyer, "if you don't know what the prices are?" One possible answer is that such a market provides the opportunity for an unscrupulous drug company to engage in chicanery of a nearly unlimited variety.

A company, we may venture to say, like TAP Pharmaceuticals. A federal investigation into TAP's pricing and marketing practices began in 1997, when Joseph Gerstein, MD, who at the time was in charge of making decisions about which drugs should be included in the formulary of a large Massachusetts HMO, came forward with his story: A TAP representative had offered him a $20,000 "educational grant" to reverse his decision not to cover TAP's prostate cancer drug, Lupron, preferring its less expensive and "therapeutically equivalent" competitor, Zoladex. "I said no. I was kind of scandalized," says Gerstein. After Gerstein started working with government investigators, TAP kept the goodies coming. "In the end," says Gerstein, "they were offering us what amounted to almost half a million dollars in various kinds of transactions that did not involve them lowering the price of Lupron. That would have queered their game with Medicare."

Medicare doesn't cover outpatient prescription drugs, but it does cover medicine, like Lupron, administered intravenously in a doctor's office. The federal program reimburses based on the doctor's own charge for the drug or on the company's list price (the AWP), whichever is lower.

According to a federal grand jury indictment, TAP representatives gave doctors all sorts of stuff—free samples, educational grants (that were in fact spent on such things as "cocktail party bar tabs" and office Christmas parties), trips to golf and ski resorts, free consulting services, medical equipment, and debt forgiveness—as inducements to use Lupron on patients with prostate cancer. In effect, docs were getting Lupron at a steeply discounted price, but the discount was hidden from the government and patients alike. The doctors were then encouraged to bill Medicare—and the men with prostate cancer who would be responsible for a 20 percent co-pay—the full AWP. Among other things, the indictment alleges that TAP's partners in crime charged patients and the federal government for thousands of free samples of Lupron. The scheme, according to the government, also defrauded Medicaid by hiding discounts to some customers and thereby skirting the requirement to offer the "best price" to the federal program for the poor.

In the end, four urologists pleaded guilty to fraud and twelve TAP managers have been indicted on multiple charges, with the latest indictments handed down July 2002. The company settled the charges by paying fines of $875 million, including the largest criminal fine ever paid in a health-care fraud case. But was TAP an isolated case? Some are skeptical. "[T]he fraud that has been exposed is only the tip of the iceberg," Congressman Pete Stark (D–CA) said when the settlement was announced in October 2001. "Investigation after investigation has identified rampant abuse of the AWP."

There's speculation based on new subpoenas to PBMs that the TAP investigation has moved on to the question of whether other TAP customers colluded to defraud Medicare and Medicaid. Meanwhile a probe of several years conducted by the Philadelphia U.S. Attorney's Office into drug pricing appears to be zeroing in on similar issues, judging from subpoenas issued to drug companies and PBMs or health plans.

Of course, these cases raise a broader question: If a drug company can rip off Medicare and Medicaid by secretly rewarding doctors, HMOs, or PBMs for pushing more expensive drugs, what stops it from doing the same thing to private-sector patients? At the heart of this question is the relatively new, relatively unregulated, and relatively opaque PBM industry itself, which has sprung up in the last couple of decades to help insurers and large employers deal with the increasingly complex business of drug benefits. PBMs now administer a majority of U.S. prescriptions. So what do they do for us?

A PBM negotiates with Drugmaker A for both discounts and rebates in exchange for encouraging patients to use Drug A and not competitors in the same class. This ability to "steer" patients is what gives PBMs their power in the marketplace. It might mean putting Drug A in plan formularies, adopting a policy that Drug A will be used first for certain conditions, charging a lower co-pay for Drug A, or promising to shift Drug A's market share in the plan from, say, 40 percent to 60 percent. Under this arrangement, doctors who prescribed a drug that was not preferred might get a phone call or fax from a plan pharmacist asking them to switch patients to the favored drug.

"Switching programs" raise the hackles of those who question whether secret price negotiations ought to determine what medicines people take. James Sheehan, the assistant U.S. attorney in Philadelphia who heads that office's probe into drug pricing, says drug switching is the subject of frequent and bitter consumer complaints. Some companies, he says, have even insisted on changing patients' antidepressants, which have widely varying effects in different people. The patient may have to wait weeks to find out whether the new medicine will bring the accustomed relief without intolerable new side effects.

The idea, of course, is that the PBM switches patients to Drug A because it has won a particularly advantageous price for the drug or other drugs by the same maker. But recall that PBMs don't share the negotiated net price of any given drug with anyone—not with the employers that hire them to manage benefits, not even with prescribing doctors. So it's impossible to tell in any individual case whether a drug is the best deal for the PBM's client. Instead, a PBM could be getting big rebates that reward it for pushing the more expensive drug, not unlike the doctors in the TAP case. "That's the black box that people aren't able to see inside," says Sager. "PBMs claim that they get better prices for you by steering more people to use certain drugs. They may have created an incredibly complicated system to enrich themselves. We don't know."

This is essentially what plaintiffs claimed in a class-action lawsuit by clients of one large PBM, Merck-Medco Managed Care (renamed Medco Health Solutions). Launched in New York state in 1997, the suit argued that Medco has a fiduciary duty to its clients—an obligation to act in their best interest—and that instead, the PBM that administers drug benefits for 65 million people furthers its own concerns, sometimes at the expense of clients' well-being. Particularly at issue is Medco's relationship with its parent company, Merck & Co., Inc. Plaintiffs alleged that Medco pushes Merck products—the cholesterol-reducing blockbuster Zocor, for example—even in cases where they're more expensive. Indeed, though Merck has consistently maintained that the companies operate independently, Medco's financial filings as part of a planned (and later shelved) spin-off from the parent company acknowledged that Merck products enjoy significantly greater market share in Medco's plans than they do nationally. More surprisingly, Medco reported that even after the companies separated, its contract with Merck would have required the PBM to continue delivering disproportionate market share to Merck drugs.

A proposed settlement of the class-action suit against Medco would give plaintiffs $42.5 million, in addition to assurances that from now on the PBM will alert clients when a switch being suggested is to a drug with a higher list price and that it will supply the net price of the medicines involved. Under the settlement, Medco would admit no liability.

The bottom line: Most often, patients being steered from Zoloft to Paxil or vice versa have absolutely no way to verify that this switch is designed to benefit them, directly or indirectly, medically or financially.

Indeed, it seems some PBMs, while presenting themselves to clients as promoters of efficiency, are promoting entirely different services to big drugmakers. And what might these services entail? Help in pitching brand-name drugs to the very patients whose employers are paying the PBM to manage claims, and costs. "Access to 75,000,000 patients . . . to help you succeed 1 product at a time," one large PBM, AdvancePCS, assures pharmaceutical-company clients. "[E]very 1 benefits," it adds hopefully. Do they really? The PBM's literature on a program to distribute free samples also promises to "turn non-writers into writers for your brand" and eliminate the "shopping bag effect" at the doctor's sample closet "so new patients get *your* product rather than a handful of alternatives." In August 2002, the company announced it would use the sampling program in a major effort to promote generics and help clients save money. But a piece that same month in the *Wall Street Journal* has the firm's CEO reporting that whereas in 1995 almost all the company's profit came from employer and health-plan clients, by 2001 most of it was coming from drug companies. The *Journal* quotes the executive as insisting there "really truly" is no inherent conflict in this arrangement.

"It's amazing," says Patty Kumbera, R.Ph., a pharmacist and executive of Iowa-based Outcomes Pharmaceutical Health Care, which puts local pharmacists in charge of managing and monitoring prescription benefits for self-insured employers. "These poor employers are really very uninformed. This isn't their area of expertise, so they buy the smoke-and-mirror games that the typical PBMs sell. It does not make sense that employers or health plans are experiencing 18 to 25 percent increases in costs, yet the PBMs keep telling them how much money they're saving them."

Kumbera joins many other observers in applauding what PBMs have accomplished in making claims processing more efficient, by helping to avoid duplicate therapies, for example. "It's when they start stepping out of data management and start affecting market share that it gets real ugly," she says. "You can't wear both hats."

And yet this basic exchange—financial reward for heavier use of a given product—appears to be very well entrenched in the U.S. health-care system. When in the fall of 2002 the federal government issued guidance saying that gifts and grants to doctors or insurers aimed at inducing them to prescribe a certain drug might run afoul of anti-kickback laws, some drugmakers reacted with indignation, insisting not that such payments are rare but that they're so widespread as to be considered standard practice. According to the *New York Times*, a coalition of nineteen pharmaceutical companies argued that the proposed code of conduct is "not grounded in an understanding of industry practices."

But as taxpayers and consumers, we want to know whether industry practices serve our goal of getting the best drug at the best price. The very obscurity of goings-on between pharmaceutical companies and their buyers casts doubt on this question. Sure, PBM deal making with drugmakers wins discounts from sticker prices. But those sticker prices are rising like nobody's business. And though the drug industry has worked closely with PBMs, it has gone to battle stations over just about any political effort to pool buyers in a way that would give them leverage in the marketplace—with more transparent accounting. PhRMA has sued states that want to take over the role of negotiating drug discounts for uninsured citizens or higher rebates for Medicaid beneficiaries. Although the industry favors establishing a drug benefit under Medicare, which would produce a surge in the volume of drugs purchased, it insists the program should be run by private insurers, and not by the federal government, a very large public buyer that could hold drugmakers' feet to the fire on prices. Perhaps it should tell us something that what this industry appears to dread the most is the day it meets, across the bargaining table, the duly elected or assigned representatives of the American people.

## JACKPOT AMERICA: A GOUGER'S PARADISE

The different-prices-for-different-folks scenario within our national borders also plays out on a global scale. We Americans pay more for drugs than virtually any other people in the world, and by a hefty margin. According to one recent estimate, Italians pay 53 percent of what cash-paying Americans pay for the same brand-name drugs. The French pay 55 percent of what we pay; the Swedes, 64 percent; Germans, 65 percent; and citizens of the U.K. and Switzerland pay 69 percent of what Americans shell out. Perhaps most galling, our neighbors in Canada pay about 62 percent of what we do for the same medicines.

If you needed sixty tablets of Zocor, the popular cholesterol-reducing drug, you'd pay $43.97 in Canada—and $109.43 just across the border in the Green Mountain State of Vermont, according to a 1998 congressional report prepared for Representative Bernie Sanders (I–VT), a longtime critic of the drug industry. One hundred Relafen pills for arthritis pain would be costly in Canada at just under $60, but exorbitant in Vermont, at $120.27. Overall, the study found that the ten drugs accounting for the highest dollar sales to elderly Vermonters cost them 81 percent more than their counterparts in Canada pay for the drugs. For some other drugs, prices diverged even more wildly: in Vermont, Knoll Pharmaceuticals charged $28.27 for Synthroid, a hormone commonly used to treat thyroid disorders; Canadians got the drug for $9.25.

Why do the drug companies charge *us* so much? Because they can. People in many parts of the world are too poor to afford basic medicine; they couldn't spend hundreds or thousands of dollars a year for brand-name drugs if they wanted to. In developed nations where drugmakers might be able to find a market for higher-priced medicines, governments play a bigger role in negotiating or setting prices for all citizens the way the U.S. government does for its veterans and military. For example, about one-third of the drugs sold in Canada are bought by the government for elderly and low-income people. Other Canadians buy their own drugs or have insurance, but unlike Americans, they can all expect to pay the same relatively affordable prices. Canada's Patented Medicine Prices Review Board puts a ceiling on what manufacturers can charge. Prices for existing patented drugs can't rise faster than inflation. Most new patented medicines must be priced in the same range as other drugs to treat the same disease. And prices for new drugs judged to be medical breakthroughs can't be higher than the median price for the same drugs in a comparison "basket" of six European countries and the United States.

What is the median U.S. price for a breakthrough drug? Canadian officials have had to go through a certain amount of rigamarole just to wrest the appropriate figures from America's many-layered pricing scheme. During a talk in Washington, D.C., in 1999, Robert G. Elgie, MD, chairperson of the Canadian board, explained that in the six European countries, prices can be verified using publicly available information. "But this leaves a question about the U.S.," he said. "In the absence of a public regulatory system, how reliable is drug price information in the United States? Ironically, this debate has been fueled by pharmaceutical manufacturers who in defending price levels in the United States have argued that real prices are lower than the publicly available prices." Canadians wanted nothing to do with the inflated list price many elderly and other uninsured Americans are stuck paying. Not long after Elgie's talk, Canada switched from the U.S. retail to federal-supply-schedule prices for inclusion in its comparison basket.

With drugs available for less across the border and around the world, some Americans have been asking for years: Why not shop for medicine where it's cheap? Importing from other countries' more hospitable marketplaces the same medicines we could purchase from local wholesalers—including drugs made right here at home—is admittedly a roundabout way of achieving the savings we're after. In testimony before the U.S. Senate, Sager referred to the irony of "laundering pills through the washing machine of the Canadian price structure." Still, political resistance to establishing similar price controls in the United States is intense, and reimportation can moderate prices. European countries like Germany and England do it. In the U.K., at least one in eight prescriptions under the National Health Service is filled by imports from countries such as France and Spain, where drugs are cheaper. This saves the government over $130 million a year, according to London's *Financial Times*.

But here we run into another special feature of the drug industry: Only manufacturers, and not wholesalers or pharmacies, are permitted to bring medicines across the border for sale in the United States. Think of it this way: Not only are we charged sharply steeper prices in our town, we're also not allowed to bring home medicines purchased at the discount store in the next town over. "Access, access, access," says PhRMA's web site; it's one of the industry group's favorite buzzwords. But PhRMA apparently means that taxpayers and insurers should free up whatever funds are necessary to facilitate the purchase of high-priced drugs, not that Americans should have access to lower-cost alternatives. The industry's position on reimportation is that it's "dangerous," a message it spread using full-page ads and intense lobbying in its 2000 effort to prevent passage of a reimportation law.

Theoretically, the drug industry lost. But the law has never been implemented. Known as the Medicine Equity and Drug Safety Act, it charged the FDA with determining whether the safety of drugs could be maintained under the new system and whether cost savings would result; Donna Shalala and, later, Tommy Thompson, Health and Human Services (HHS) secretaries under the Clinton and Bush administrations, both announced the FDA could not meet these requirements. Supporters of reimportation are exasperated by these safety concerns: No, you can't guarantee against adulterated drugs crossing the border, but neither can you guarantee drugs won't be tampered with inside the United States, nor can anyone give 100-percent assurance against contamination of other products we import—food, for example. The law would have allowed reimportation only of FDA-approved medicines manufactured in the United States and a limited set of other approved countries. Importers would have been required to test drugs for quality and keep close track of where they came from. Still, even leaving aside questions of safety and quality control, the law had problems. Consumers Union, the nonprofit publisher of *Consumer Reports,* pointed out a provision that effectively barred the whole process: Importers would have to obtain FDA-approved labels from manufacturers, and manufacturers could simply refuse to provide them. And even if wholesalers did get clearance to sell imported drugs, there was no guarantee they'd pass the savings on to Todd Pelletier and Melva McCuddy.

Then there's the question of whether the industry would simply adapt to reimportation by drying up the supply of drugs to wholesalers in places where medicines are cheaper. In late 2001, GlaxoSmithKline announced it would limit supplies to European wholesalers so they'd have only enough to meet local demand, thereby thwarting U.K. pharmacies' attempts to buy cheaper medicines abroad. This move may well run afoul of the European Commission, which expressly approves parallel imports as part of the establishment of a single economy. Pharmaceutical executives have strenuously argued against the coupling of cross-continent free trade with national price controls, a system that, as Sager suggested, allows one country to "import" a dose of another's pricing policy.

In the summer of 2002, the Senate passed a bill allowing U.S. reimportation of drugs from Canada alone, but with the same deal-breaking caveat as the 2000 legislation: The secretary of Health and Human Services would have to agree that the strategy poses no risk to consumers, an invitation HHS head Tommy Thompson has already once declined. *Investor's Business Daily* headlined its report on the new legislation, "Why Drug Firms Don't Worry over Cheap Canadian Resales." With new versions of reimportation on the table, the fight in Congress isn't over yet. In the meantime, a growing number of Americans who aren't rich enough to pay the world's highest prices—but need their meds now—are taking the matter into their own hands.

They're simply "importing" a personal supply of the drugs they need. Politicians from Northern states such as Montana, Maine, Minnesota, and Vermont have sponsored numerous "drug runs" to Canada, having found no better way to dramatize the issue of high drug prices than the spectacle of elderly Americans climbing aboard buses bound for Canadian border towns where pharmacies have taken to hanging out shingles: "We fill American prescriptions." But these trips aren't just for show. An unknown but apparently substantial number of people go to Canada regularly and depend on the savings they get there.

Some go on their own. Others have hooked up with bus operations like Pharmtrip, launched in Springfield, Ohio, in 2000 by former hospital administrator David Moses. Every year, several hundred local people get medicine through Pharmtrip, which is for-profit but not yet breaking even, says Moses. Johanne and Edd McCracken go every three months. The trip is perhaps seven hours, and when they get there, says Johanne, they wait in line for the pharmacist to match their medications to their name tags. "It's a regular pharmacy and there's all these people coming in that live there getting their prescriptions," she says. "They just look at you like, 'What are you doing here?' It's not very private, but it saves us money. We have to do what we have to do to save money." Both McCrackens have diabetes and high blood pressure, and Johanne suffers from arthritis.

About the same time Moses was getting the idea for Pharmtrip from a local television report on bus trips to Canada from the Northeast, Vermont health-system administrator Elizabeth Wennar was riding along on one of those trips to get a sense of what it was like. "It took about twelve hours from beginning to end," she says. "It was a very hot day. I remember thinking to myself, 'How in heaven's name can these people do this?' Because all of them had some chronic disease and some of them had to be literally carried on and off the bus because of their conditions. But they were very focused on getting their medications." Meanwhile, as CEO of United Health Alliance, a system of 120 physicians and several health-care facilities in southwestern Vermont, Wennar had heard from doctors who were frustrated at writing scripts that were never filled because of cost. Wennar and the board of United Health Alliance created Medicine Assist, a not-for-profit on-line mail-order service for getting prescription drugs from Canada. The patient and doctor both download forms from the Medicine Assist web site, fill them out, and fax them, along with a prescription, to a participating pharmacy. The cost of the Canadian doctor's review is included in the prices available on the web site. Once an order is placed, the pharmacy mails the medicines straight to the patient's home.

Not surprisingly, this route has proven more popular than the bus. Indeed, the rapid growth of Medicine Assist (as well as many for-profit mail-order operations) gives you an idea of how the market might work if it were truly open, if American consumers could see where value lay and were free to seek it out. Every week, United Health Alliance receives hundreds of inquiries about Medicine Assist, which serves people in every state and Puerto Rico. Overwhelmed by the demands of the program but committed to its premise, United Health Alliance has been in negotiations to turn the operation over to a foundation that would establish a call center in Canada with 250 work stations.

There's only one problem: It's not exactly legal. The FDA allows individuals to bring in a personal supply of only those drugs that treat a serious condition and aren't available in the United States. Most personal importers don't meet these specs. Still, the agency has advised customs officers not to confiscate medicines carried across the border if they're clearly for personal use and no more than a ninety-day supply, says Tom McGinnis, FDA director of pharmacy affairs.

"We're a little bit more concerned about mail order," says McGinnis. FDA policy calls for detaining international shipments of prescription drugs, but in practice, this policy can be carried out only sporadically. Indeed, while drugmakers protest their concern for Americans' safety should reimportation be legalized, the truth is, the government today has very little power to stop the gray market in prescription drugs. Medicines are being shipped to Americans from all over the world, often ordered from 1 of 200-some international web sites, many of which don't even require a prescription. In a 2001 pilot survey at a postal facility in Carson City, California, FDA inspectors worked forty hours a week examining packages—far more time than is normally possible—

and still were able to check only a fraction of eligible shipments. During the five-week survey, inspectors detained 721 packages from nineteen countries. About 8 percent contained drugs with no labeling. A few contained drugs that had been withdrawn from the U.S. market because of safety problems, and others contained potentially addictive medications. The many seniors who just want to get heart medicine at a price they can afford venture into this world with understandable trepidation and are fortunate to find a service like Medicine Assist, which involves full participation by the patient's personal physician, and known medicines from known sources.

For her part, Wennar would welcome FDA oversight of Medicine Assist and thinks it could be achieved through a licensing system for Canadian pharmacies. "Do I believe personal importation is the perfect answer? No," says Wennar. "But it is working in the meantime. All we ask is just step out of our way and let us continue doing the right thing for the right reasons."

There are signs that rebellion against the reimportation ban is growing. Saying the move was merely an attempt to clarify policy on drugs bought by travelers, insurer United-Health Group Inc. sent letters in the fall of 2002 to 97,000 members of its AARP drug-discount plan announcing it would reimburse them for medicines they purchase outside the country. Wennar's United Health Alliance recently surveyed pharmacies in all Canadian provinces (most of them unaffiliated with Medicine Assist) and added up the number of Americans they're already serving. An astonishing 1.1 million.

# [chapter 2]

# PATENT SHENANIGANS

To keep selling brand-name drugs at premium prices, manufacturers have to prevent consumers from getting access to controlled foreign markets—and they have to prevent low-cost alternatives from competing in the U.S. market. In the latter case, patents are their most important tool.

A patent rewards a brand-name company for investing in the development of a drug by giving that company the exclusive right to sell its new product for a period of time. Technically, the term is twenty years, but this is subject to many variables. Since original patents are usually issued well before a drug reaches the market, the so-called effective patent life may be substantially shorter. On the other hand, as we shall see, drugmakers avail themselves of various methods to extend patent life or to protect an exclusive market beyond the expiration of primary patents. There's much at stake in this push-pull. When a brand-name medicine loses legal protection for its monopoly, other companies can make and sell generic copies of the drug.

This moment can usher in enormous savings for consumers. A 1998 Congressional Budget Office (CBO) study found that brand-name manufacturers tend to raise the price of new medicines as they gain acceptance and to keep raising prices even after similar brand-name medicines come on the market. By contrast, the first generic that becomes available is usually 20 to 30 percent cheaper than its branded equivalent. When (and if) additional generic products enter the fray, fierce price competition ensues, and generic prices drop to one-third of the brand-name price. Brand-name companies don't participate in this race to the bottom—in fact they may raise prices, relying on a few brand loyalists to pay even more.

Loyalists notwithstanding, the outcome of a generic launch is all but inevitable. Even if the brand-name's maker can convince doctors to keep writing scripts for the more expensive product, druggists in most states are allowed to substitute the generic. Brand-name sales typically drop like a stone—ultimately by about 75 percent, according to the *Wall Street Journal*. One prominent example: When the colossally successful antidepressant Prozac went off-patent in August 2001, Prozac Nation quickly gave way to its generic equivalent, fluoxetine nation. U.S. Prozac sales plummeted 80 percent between first-quarter 2001 and first-quarter 2002. Overall U.S. sales for Prozac's maker, Eli Lilly and Company, fell 16 percent. And Lilly stock took a hit, losing about one-fourth of its value. Of course patent expirations are entirely expected and accounted for in the long-range planning of industry executives and stock watchers. Still, when a blockbuster drug—the kind that wows Wall Street and gets top billing in annual reports—loses patent protection, it's a dark day for the drug's maker.

In response, drug companies are devising ever more ingenious ways to extend their products' exclusive hold on the market. The practice known as "evergreening" takes many forms, but the gist is this: Just as a lucrative product is about to go off-patent, the company claims some new basis for keeping the monopoly alive. It may list new patents on the same drug—patents that claim proprietary rights to the way the drug is manufactured, say, or to its inactive ingredients. Or it puts out the same drug in a new formulation: a timed-release version, for example, or a pill that combines the drug with another existing drug. These forms can proliferate into whole "families" related to the "mother drug." The original patent still expires, but the tweaked versions can't be sold in generic form for another three years. A company can also claim new uses for the drug: In addition to an indication for depression, it's now proven to work for, say, bulimia. That means that generic companies can sell copies of the brand-name drug but won't be able to use labeling that claims the new use for a period of three years; the drugs may not be listed as equivalent, preventing substitution at many pharmacies. In other cases, companies patent an extremely close chemical relative of the lucrative drug and launch a "new and improved" product, under a different name: Clarinex instead of Claritin, Nexium instead of Prilosec.

Some new patents are of course legitimate. Certainly, incremental changes to existing drugs or research establishing new uses can benefit patients. Two questions come to mind, though. When does a company's right to monopolize its essential innovation come to a legitimate end? And how in the world are consumers—who only want to know what specific benefits are available in various products, and at what price—supposed to beat their way through *this* thicket?

The more egregious forms of evergreening, smacking of anticompetitive manipulation, have provoked wide-ranging investigations by the Federal Trade Commission (FTC) and state attorneys general. "They're keeping us very busy in antitrust divisions across the country," says Meredyth Smith Andrus, a Maryland assistant attorney general who co-chairs a national drug-pricing task force of state attorneys general staff. Although a company may lose its patent fight in the end, says Andrus, extending the franchise on a big seller for even a few months can mean many millions of dollars in revenue. "Often it appears to be a business decision on the part of the pharmaceutical company: How long can I prevent generic competition, charge this price, and get away with it? Ultimately I'm going to have to pay for it, but is it worth it?"

Ironically, drugmakers have been eking out those extra months and years in part by exploiting a law created to encourage entry of generics into the market. The Drug Price Competition and Patent Term Restoration Act of 1984 (called "Hatch-Waxman" after its sponsors on Capitol Hill) simplified requirements for FDA approval of generic drugs. Under the law, rather than filing a new application, complete with research proving safety and efficacy, generics manufacturers are allowed to rely on the brand-name companies' data. All the generics company has to do is prove its drug is "bioequivalent" to the brand-name drug, that is, demonstrate that it contains the same active ingredient and is absorbed by the body at the same rate and to the same extent. Hatch-Waxman virtually created the U.S. generics market. Before the law was enacted, sales of a brand-name drug might continue more or less unchallenged for years after patent expiration. Since its inception, generics prescriptions have more than doubled, accounting for 45 percent of scripts written by U.S. doctors. The law also succeeded in protecting brand-name companies' impetus for innovation. It granted patent extensions to restore time lost in development and regulatory review (when the drug would be patented but not on the market producing revenue). And it gave brand companies three years' exclusive right to market a new indication or form of an existing drug. Around the mid-1980s, the average effective patent life of a new drug was 8.1 years. By the late 1990s, thanks to Hatch-Waxman and other regulatory changes, branded drugs could expect to maintain patent protection for, on average, 13.9 to 15.4 years.

In theory, the Hatch-Waxman balance looked like this: Brand-name drugs would enjoy longer periods of market monopoly and produce more revenue for their makers, but after their patents expired, one or more generics would appear with all due speed on pharmacy shelves.

But there's a loophole in the law: If a generics manufacturer announces plans to market a drug for which a brand-name company holds a patent, the brand-name company can sue and get an *automatic thirty-month stay* against the generic. The brand company doesn't have to make a case for the stay. Simply by filing the suit, it stops the generic from entering the market for at least two and a half years. Moreover, no regulatory gatekeeper assesses the validity of patents before they're listed. "It might be something that wouldn't do well in court," says Patrick Cafferty, an attorney with Miller Faucher and Cafferty, LLP, who has been active in litigation against drug companies. "But in practice," he says, "it's a unilateral process. There's nobody opposing the party seeking the patent." This arrangement, critics say, has allowed brand companies to block generic entry by cramming the FDA's "Orange Book" with late-listed or bogus patents, which then form the basis of patent-infringement cases against firms trying to sell a generic.

Another legal provision gives the first company to apply for FDA approval to market a generic six months in which no other generic can come to market. This compensates the first generics company for facing litigation and other risks associated with leading the way. But it also means that if a brand-name company can keep the first generic applicant at bay, it stalls all generic competition, sometimes indefinitely.

The FTC conducted a thorough review of this litigation in 2001, issuing its report in July 2002. It found that in 75 out of 104 cases where a generics company applied to market a product it claimed did not infringe a brand-name patent (or when it claimed the brand patent was invalid), the brand-name pharmaceutical company sued. If it sued the first generic applicant, it very likely sued the second as well. In three-fourths of the cases that had been decided by a court, the generic applicant had ultimately prevailed. "The data," according to the FTC report, "suggest that the generic applicants have brought appropriate patent challenges."

Brand and generic drugmakers have waged an ardent struggle over rights to market omeprazole, a generic version of Prilosec, originally slated to lose patent protection in October 2001. In addition to bringing Nexium on board, maker AstraZeneca filed at least six patents to supplement the original. Those patents have been the basis for lawsuits against a veritable army of generics companies waiting to bring copies of the brand-name drug to market. "It costs a hundred and fifty bucks to file, and certainly they have legal fees. But Prilosec is worth 11 million dollars a day," says Cafferty. "That's why they're fighting so hard for every day." AstraZeneca appeared to have won a critical victory in October 2002, when a federal judge ruled that the first generic applicants to the FDA infringed "formulation" patents covering a subcoating between the active drug in Prilosec and its outer layer. But the court found that a third generic company, the German Kremers Urban Development Company (Kudco) did not violate the patent.

Thus, more than a year after the main patent expired, a generic version of Prilosec was cleared for U.S. takeoff. Because the patent system is rife with opportunities for such wrangling, the brand-name company and its generic rivals spent resources in litigation that might have gone toward drug development or might have allowed lower prices for consumers. AstraZeneca made some billions on its purple pill during the delay, and, critically, bought itself time to convert patients to its new purple pill, Nexium, launched in 2001.

Or look at the antidepressant Paxil. The patent Glaxo-SmithKline (GSK) holds on the active ingredient is scheduled to expire in 2006. In the decade 1988–1998, it listed no new patents in the FDA's Orange Book for Paxil. Then Apotex, a generic drug company, applied to market a slightly different version of paroxetine; it claims this version does not violate the Paxil patent, an issue that has yet to be decided in court. The FDA tentatively approved Apotex's application in May 2001. But in the meantime, GSK listed nine new patents in the Orange Book and, based on those new patents, filed five new patent-infringement cases against Apotex, and several more against other generics firms. According to Canadian patent attorney Shonagh McVean, who has represented Apotex and helped prepare materials on Paxil for the FTC, the new patents cover methods for making Paxil, different forms of Paxil, and new uses unapproved by the FDA, such as the use of Paxil to treat premenstrual disorder when symptoms include "anger, rejection sensitivity and lack of mental or physical energy." Whether or not these patents are valid, each of GSK's lawsuits against generics firms triggers a thirty-month stay, blocking generic entry through at least 2003. "With respect to all the pending litigation in the USA relating to Paxil, the Group believes that its patents are valid and that the third party compounds do infringe the Group's patents, and it intends to vigorously litigate its position," GSK told shareholders in a recent annual report. In December 2002, a court ruled one contested Paxil patent invalid, upheld another, and in two other patents validated some claims while rejecting others. Paxil sales, meanwhile, climbed to more than $2 billion a year.

But litigation is not the only, and perhaps not even the most important way to shore up a brand-name market against competitors. During the last several years, GSK has also won FDA approval for new uses of Paxil, which help extend and sustain the franchise. Originally approved to treat depression, the drug now has approval for obsessive-compulsive disorder, panic disorder, and post-traumatic stress disorder. After Paxil became the first drug approved to treat a rare and extreme form of shyness, called social anxiety disorder (SAD), in 1999, GSK struck out to raise awareness about SAD, and stories suddenly proliferated in popular media. "Some people find comfort just by learning social anxiety is a medical condition," GlaxoSmithKline's web site, www.Paxil.com, informs browsers. "Learning more about your condition is often a good first step toward feeling better." The web site includes a questionnaire to help people determine whether they have SAD and lists resources for finding a physician. In 2001, Paxil became the only drug in its class—selective serotonin reuptake inhibitors, or SSRIs—approved for use in generalized anxiety disorder. And in mid-2002 GSK launched Paxil CR, a slow-release form of the blockbuster drug.

In some cases, protecting market share for a top-selling "mother" drug involves getting patients to switch to one of its offspring. The new dosage form may be more convenient, perhaps better tolerated. But what drug companies won't point out to patients is that the new version is invariably more expensive than the generic that may now compete with its mother drug. For example, patients on the diabetes drug Glucophage, which recently lost patent protection, can now choose a generic equivalent. In question-and-answer format, Bristol-Myers Squibb Company's web site explains the "difference" between its Glucophage and the generic drug metformin: "*What about cost?* For people without insurance, a prescription drug plan, or Medicaid, generic substitutes are usually less expensive. However, people with insurance, a prescription drug plan, or Medicaid typically see little or no cost difference." (They don't *see* the difference, but it's there.) The web site also advises patients to be vigilant about substitution at the drugstore: "[R]emember, the choice is up to you and your doctor." But for those who've switched to the new Glucophage XR, a timed-release version you don't have to take as often, there can be no substitution: "*I take Glucophage XR. Does this information apply to me?* No. There is no generic equivalent for Glucophage XR available." The new, timed-release version is priced a bit lower per prescription than the standard Glucophage. Another Glucophage baby, Glucovance, combines the mother drug with a generic diabetes medicine.

Not long before Prozac was due to lose patent protection, Lilly repackaged the drug in pastel colors and began marketing it to women as Sarafem, indicated for the treatment of premenstrual dysphoric disorder (PMDD), a controversial diagnosis for a severe form of various physical and especially mental premenstrual symptoms. The company web site claims that "millions of menstruating women" suffer from the problem. A highlighted box seems designed to guard against substitution with generic fluoxetine, telling women to "make sure" that "the prescription you receive says 'Sarafem'" and "the 20-mg Sarafem capsule is lavender and pink." A search of www.drugstore.com turns up a price of just over a dollar per capsule for generic fluoxetine—and about $3 per pill for the pink-and-lavender capsule. The drug achieved sales of only $85 million in 2001; in late 2002, Lilly sold the U.S. marketing rights to Sarafem to Galen Holdings, PLC, a pharmaceutical company based in Craigavon, Northern Ireland. "The increasing awareness of PMDD amongst the medical community presents us with a great opportunity to develop this recently launched product," Galen's CEO said in a press release. Recently *re*launched, he might have said.

The patent on Claritin, the multibillion-dollar antihista-

mine, was set to expire at the end of 2002. But maker Schering-Plough also holds a patent on a metabolite of Claritin's
active ingredient, that is, on a substance the body makes in
response to taking Claritin. Enter Clarinex, a purified version of the metabolite, approved in late 2001 with spanking
new patents that extend to the year 2019 (though it's not
clear how long they would bar generic competition).
"They're pushing it with unbelievable venom," says Gerstein, the whistle-blower in the TAP case. "Every physician's
office is full of samples. Right now it costs slightly less than
Claritin. And it's all done at the tail end of the patent status
of Claritin so that when it finally goes off-patent there will
be millions of people on Clarinex." Meanwhile, Claritin
would be launched as an over-the-counter drug, to be sold
at a fraction of its former prescription-only price.

Some drugmakers, faced with the seemingly inevitable
launch of a generic rival, have apparently given the would-
be competitor cash to back off. Maryland's Andrus calls
such arrangements a "new animal" in the antitrust world.
In one case some thirty attorneys general alleged that Bristol-Myers Squibb (BMS) settled its own patent-infringement suit against a generics company by essentially paying
the company $72 million to hold off marketing a generic
version of anti-anxiety med BuSpar. BMS was also accused
of filing a sham patent on BuSpar, even as one generics firm
had its competing product loaded on trucks and ready for
market (while denying the charges, the company agreed to
settle this and related BuSpar litigation for $535 million in
early 2003). Consumers represented by the Boston-based
Prescription Access Litigation (PAL) project have sued Bayer
AG and three generics makers, claiming that Bayer paid the

generics manufacturers to refrain from challenging its patent on top-selling antibiotic Cipro. In a third case, PAL, joined this time by lawyers from the seniors advocate AARP, allege the makers of breast-cancer drug Nolvadex (tamoxifen) colluded with generics maker Barr Laboratories to inflate the price of tamoxifen by keeping true generic versions off the market. Instead of challenging the Nolvadex patent, the suit alleges, Barr agreed to license tamoxifen from its maker Zeneca (now AstraZeneca) for resale as a "generic" whose price is only 5 percent less than AstraZeneca's brand-name drug.

Recall that because of its claim to six months' market exclusivity, if the first generics applicant to the FDA opts not to go to market, it effectively blocks other generic products from doing so. Thus, agreements between brand-name and generic drugmakers are essentially a way of "sharing the monopoly," as Cafferty puts it. The smaller company abandons the risk of litigation for a bird in hand, and the brand-name company pays a small price to maintain control of a cash cow.

Efforts have been afoot in Congress to close loopholes in Hatch-Waxman, including a proposal approved by the Senate in 2002 that would do away with the automatic thirty-month stay for patents listed months or years after the original drug approval. Instead, brand companies (like litigants in other situations) would have to go to court and convince a judge that a stay is justified. Such proposals are, not surprisingly, anathema to the drug industry. Speaking to reporters early in 2002, PhRMA's Richard I. Smith vowed to oppose the reopening of Hatch-Waxman, based on what he called "a handful of anecdotes" about delays in generics firms' ability to market their products. Then, out of the blue and only weeks before the November 2002 midterm election, President George W. Bush, on whom the industry had relied for support, proposed new FDA rules limiting drug companies to one thirty-month stay against a generic competitor over a particular drug. The rules would also try to block companies from filing patents for trivial product attributes like packaging. The industry stayed mum immediately following the announcement; some observers predicted drugmakers would sue over the rules, which in any case would be expected to hand consumers more modest savings than are held out by the Senate bill.

If Hatch-Waxman provides Big Pharma with a main thoroughfare to patent extension, then the legal incentive known as "pediatric exclusivity" is at least an important side street. The industry has fought hard to keep it open. Adopted in 1997 and renewed in 2001 over the protests of some consumer groups, the law gives a company six months' extra patent time on a drug it agrees to test in children. This incentive has stimulated hundreds of pediatric drug studies, but it has also brought a huge windfall to drug companies that use the provision to extend patents on major blockbusters—including drugs for hypertension, arthritis, and heartburn.

The children's trials themselves cost a few million dollars at most. By contrast, the *Wall Street Journal* estimates six-month patent extensions have helped Schering-Plough pull in an extra $975 million on Claritin, Bristol-Myers Squibb make an additional $648 million on Glucophage, and Eli Lilly boost Prozac revenues by $831 million. Twelve out of nineteen drugs with sales over $1 billion in 1999 were slated to receive patent extensions for pediatric testing, reports Public Citizen, the thirty-year-old consumer advocacy group founded by Ralph Nader.

The paucity of drug research on kids is a long-standing problem. Drugmakers have been reluctant to take on the complexities of pediatric trials, especially since the market for adult drugs is much more substantial. As a result, doctors often have to prescribe for kids by extrapolating from data on adults, even though children often respond quite differently. To many children's health advocates, the trade-off of patent life for research is a good one. "I think what's happened is that the incentives have worked first for the large-market drugs," says Susan Weiner, president of The Children's Cause, an advocacy group for kids with cancer. "But the law has changed the internal priorities of companies in a way that is favorable for our kids. The utility of cancer drugs for kids is at least being discussed, whereas five years ago that really wasn't the case."

Others argue that companies selling drugs of great potential utility in children ought to be required to do the tests in the first place. "I think the incentive will actually lead to putting off pediatric studies," says the University of Minnesota's Schondelmeyer. "The drug companies will wait until near the end of the patent life of the drug. And when do we need these studies? Soon after the drug comes on the market."

Proposals to trim the incentive when it was up for renewal in 2001 were defeated by industry lobbying that one health advocate calls "thuggish." According to John Golenski, Ed.D., who was active on the issue as head of a consortium of business, union, and consumer groups formed to address the problem of high prescription drug costs, "They basically said, 'If you guys push for any changes, we'll kill it altogether,'" an outcome dreaded by child-health advocates who had worked so long to encourage more research. As PhRMA spokesperson Jeff Trewhitt told the AARP *Bulletin*, "If it ain't broke, don't fix it."

# [chapter 3]

## YOU SAY PROFITS, THEY SAY R&D

"AMERICA'S Pharmaceutical Companies: New Medicines. New Hope." This is the tag line for the recent full-page ads appearing in national magazines as part of PhRMA's campaign to gussy up its increasingly negative image. The ads feature handsome, smiling people in lab coats—just some of the "50,000 researchers at America's pharmaceutical companies [who are] dedicating their lives to making all our lives better." Readers are directed to a web site, www.newmedicines.org, where they can learn about products these scientists are working to develop. Perusing its promotional materials, you might get the idea the pharmaceutical industry is a nonprofit research operation out to save the human race by putting every disease that afflicts us "on the path to extinction," as one industry spokesperson put it.

But this message of hope has a dark side. Faced with a proposal to limit drug prices, industry representatives invariably respond by insisting the measure will put an end to research into terrifying diseases like Alzheimer's and cancer, hitting us where we live. In a statement to reporters this year, PhRMA's Smith warned that efforts to reform Hatch-Waxman "would seriously erode the incentive and protection for innovation that enables new drug development, and would be a devastating blow to America's patients." It's as if without the advantage of the thirty-month stay, drugmakers wouldn't be motivated to come up with new products. "And I guarantee you," Smith went on, "if you aren't already today, at some point in your lives every one in this room will be a patient in need of medical care. The question is: Will a medicine be there for you?"

This is the industry driving home its message, "'If you touch our profits, the laboratories will close and you'll all die,'" says Boston University's Sager. "It's a terror tactic."

Certainly, pharmaceutical companies take on risk by spending very large sums in their laboratories. Comparing numbers from PhRMA's annual member survey with government appropriations, the Federation of American Societies for Experimental Biology (FASEB) estimates that big pharmaceutical companies sponsored 47 percent of all biomedical research and development, or "R&D," in 2000. This represented a huge increase in R&D spending by PhRMA in the latter half of the decade, with the government's share of total R&D declining to 39 percent, despite substantial increases in the National Institutes of Health (NIH) budget.

But some frankly doubt PhRMA's figures, derived from confidential reports by member companies. Indeed, the subject of who spends what on R&D, like the question of who pays what for drugs, must remain murky: Although pharma execs hold up R&D spending as a justification for just about everything they do, they hold the details of this spending very close to the chest. Examinations by various advocacy groups of drugmakers' financial reports have yielded much lower estimates of their R&D budgets. For example, whereas manufacturers reported spending over $20 billion on R&D in 1999, Sager and colleague Deborah Socolar, MPH, arrived at "a more skeptical estimate," based on financial filings, of about $10 billion.

Also a matter for dispute is the industry claim that it costs, on average, $802 million to develop a drug today, up from $231 million at the beginning of the decade. These numbers come from the nonprofit Tufts Center for the Study of Drug Development, whose work, in part industry funded, is often cited by industry leaders to support arguments about the risks of R&D. The $802-million figure was unveiled at a press conference in the fall of 2001. Merck's CEO spoke, heralding the findings as confirmation of the increasingly complex nature of drug development. The Tufts Center's director said the new data demonstrate that drug companies' "single largest challenge" is to contain the cost of R&D. But outsiders couldn't verify the validity of the data, proprietary information provided to the Tufts researchers by ten big drug companies. They couldn't even examine the study itself, which was still being submitted to peer review for publication in a research journal. In fact, a year later the study remained unavailable to the public, though the rather shocking figure it generated—$802 million—is widely disseminated.

This number is "on steroids," according to Jamie Love, an economist and head of the Consumer Project on Technology, founded by Ralph Nader. It describes the costs of development for a select group of the most innovative drugs. And it includes money a drug company actually lays out to take a new medicine from discovery to human trials, money it spends on drugs that don't pan out, plus—here's the controversial part—money the company might have earned had it invested its R&D funds elsewhere. This last, known as the "cost of capital," accounts for roughly half the $802 million figure. Moreover, although the study authors attribute much of the increase in R&D costs to higher costs for human drug trials, Love is convinced the Tufts researchers grossly exaggerate this. He points out that for one category of drugs—"orphan" drugs to treat rare diseases—drug companies reported in recent tax filings that they spent on average $7.9 million for clinical trials.

A study by the Global Alliance for TB Drug Development released around the same time as the Tufts study put the cost of drug development at between $40 million and $125 million, including the cost of research "dry holes," but not the lost opportunity for investment returns elsewhere.

Perhaps more important than the question of exactly what companies spend on R&D—assume it's a large and increasing amount—is the issue of what these drug-development dollars are yielding. After all, in asserting the need to charge high prices for drugs, industry spokespeople implicitly suggest that their R&D has enormous social value—that it proffers "new hope" to the sick and dying. And indeed, few would deny that the history of the pharmaceutical industry is, in part, the history of human progress: From vaccines to antibiotics and, more recently, an array of cardiovascular drugs, some medicines have produced benefits beyond measure. But brush aside the industry platitudes about new cures for a close look at products coming though R&D pipelines, and you'll find that often their value is more commercial than social.

Of all the drugs approved in the United States between 1989 and 2000, only 15 percent were made of new ingredients deemed by the FDA to provide significant clinical benefit over drugs already on the market, according to a NIHCM study released in May 2002. Well over half the drugs approved during these twelve years were "product-line extensions" using old active ingredients. As the pace of new drug approvals accelerated sharply over the last decade, "standard-rated" product-line extensions—those adding no significant benefit—accounted for 62 percent of this growth. Although clearly less expensive to develop than more innovative drugs, these standard-rated product-line extensions also contributed most to increased consumer spending on new drugs in the five years leading up to 2000. In other words, the NIHCM numbers reveal changes clearly related to the trend that has patent lawyers so busy: Drug companies are flooding the market with new dosages, new combinations, and otherwise rejiggered forms of older medicines.

These product-line extensions are different from the so-called me-too drugs, a term used to describe the many new drugs that are chemically distinct from those already on the market but mimic their basic mechanism of action. There are, for example, numerous selective serotonin reuptake inhibitors to treat depression, cholesterol-reducing statins, and proton pump inhibitors for ulcers. Sometimes, a drug company is encouraged by competitors' market success to develop a me-too drug. Its me-too may be safer, more effective, or produce fewer side effects than forerunners. Other times, the company doesn't intend its product to be a me-too; it's just that some other firm beats it to the market. "Nobody wants to make a me-too drug," says Robert Ehrlich, CEO of Rx Insight, which supports the industry with consulting on marketing to consumers. "They'll market them because getting any share in a big category is profitable. But ideally if you're developing a new drug, you want a drug that clearly meets an unmet demand, and ideally in a large population."

Drugmakers would be delighted to produce an out-and-out miracle every six months. Unfortunately, big breakthroughs are few and far between and not entirely predictable. Meanwhile, the industry's need to produce revenue never lets up.

Generally speaking, the drug industry does not expend resources to develop medicines that might be an enormous boon for public health but offer little prospect for commercial gain. A tiny percentage of new drugs brought to market are designed to treat diseases like malaria that kill huge numbers of poor people around the world. "That market is perceived as not very rewarding," says Polly Harrison, Ph.D., head of the business, research, and advocacy consortium Alliance for Microbicide Development. "The products need to be subsidized by the public sector—World Bank, USAID, UNICEF. There's a negotiated bulk price, which you would think would be rewarding because of large volume but has not been understood to be rewarding."

Harrison and other public-health advocates have been trying for years to get money to develop gels women could apply vaginally to protect themselves from sexually transmitted diseases, including HIV. The London School of Hygiene and

Tropical Medicine has estimated that such a product could avert between 2.5 and 3.7 million new cases of HIV infection worldwide within three years. Researchers have identified three promising products, but the clinical trials needed to prove preventive, as opposed to curative, effects are expensive. The Rockefeller Foundation and the Bill and Melinda Gates Foundation have stepped up with support, as have the NIH and other public entities. So far, large drug companies have stayed away. "We haven't been able to address Big Pharma," says Michael Harper, MD, director of the Consortium for Industrial Collaboration in Contraceptive Research (CICCR), a major actor in the microbicides field. "They've said, 'If you get something that would be great, but it's just not in our corporate game plan.'"

The *Wall Street Journal* recently reported on a promising treatment for sepsis, a runaway infection that kills 215,000 Americans a year. One study in France showed that patients given low-dose steroids for septic shock were 29 percent less likely to die from the episode. That the drugs are off-patent and less than $50 a dose seems a major plus for patients who might benefit from the treatment, but it deters drug companies from doing the research needed to prove the approach works. The University of Tennessee doctor who stumbled on the treatment had to rely on a church-affiliated hospital chain to fund a small study. Meanwhile, the *Journal* reports, Eli Lilly paid 250 critical-care specialists to speak to their colleagues about its new $7,000-a-dose sepsis drug, Xigris.

Indeed, some argue that our national research agenda—especially when it comes to private-sector research, but also including the public sector—places too much emphasis on the biomedical studies needed to bring forth potentially profitable new drugs and far too little on examining how the drugs we have can be used to best effect in American communities. One example: Many more kids are taking psychoactive medications than in the past. A January 2003 University of Maryland study documented a two- to three-fold increase between 1987 and 1996 in the percentage of American children using these medications, including stimulants to treat attention deficit hyperactivity disorder, antidepressants, and drugs for anxiety and psychotic disorders, sometimes in combination. This trend appears to have continued through 2000, according to the study's principal author, Julie Magno Zito, Ph.D. What does it mean? It's a bit like a Rorschach. Some experts are inclined to see an encouraging movement toward noticing and treating children's psychiatric problems; others see a worrisome tendency to overdiagnose those ills or to choose the expediency of medication over more complex approaches to problematic behavior. Zito herself sees a knowledge vacuum. Where the drugs have been studied in kids, she says, "you're generally only doing a drug-placebo comparison and you're focused on symptom improvement over a relatively short period of time," sixteen weeks perhaps. This sort of study doesn't tell you what the symptoms mean for a child's life functioning or how the drugs affect the development of children who take them for years. It doesn't begin to assess the extensive and diverse real-world circumstances in which these drugs are now being used. Zito remarks, "We really should be doing much more creative work showing—in the children—the benefits compared to existing drugs or compared to non-drug conditions and psychotherapy."

If it seems natural that drug companies don't volunteer to bankroll research that's unlikely to benefit their bottom line—they're businesses after all, not public health activists—then perhaps it will seem more surprising that taxpayers support a portion of the research to develop drugs over which drug companies claim sole proprietorship. Proprietorship, and, of course, the right to charge whatever they please.

"If you call up and ask the company did the government help in the development of this drug, they will say no," says Love. The feds aren't keeping score, either. But it's clear that public support is critical, especially to the development of truly innovative drugs for serious illnesses. In the early 1990s, Love and his colleagues did an in-depth study tracking the history of thirty innovative and important drugs approved between 1987 and 1991. They found that half these drugs had been developed with help from the federal government. For eleven of the drugs, the federal government had been involved at every stage of development, from discovery to human trials. Of particular interest: The government-funded drugs were significantly *more* expensive than other medicines. In 1993 testimony to the U.S. Senate, Love and Ralph Nader reported that the National Cancer Institute (NCI) supported human trials on 92 percent of cancer drugs developed since 1955. (Indeed, in its www.newmedicines.com web site, the industry touts seventy drugs now in development for women's cancers; for twenty-four of these, the web site lists under the heading "company" none other than the National Cancer Institute.) In 1998, the *Boston Globe* took a close look at thirty-five important—and top-selling—drugs the FDA had approved over the previous five years: All but two of them had been brought through the R&D pipeline with the help of NIH or FDA funds.

And what do taxpayers get in exchange? Well they get a new medicine. The question is whether they can afford to use it. According to a report by Representative Bernie Sanders' office, the tamoxifen that costs Canadians about $34 per treatment sets back an American cash-paying patient more than $240—and was the product of 140 clinical trials sponsored by *our* government. "It is absurd that Americans must pay twice for lifesaving drugs, first as taxpayers to develop the drug and then as consumers to pad pharmaceutical profits," says Sanders.

Uncle Sam more or less encourages university researchers and drug companies to take the money and run. Twenty years ago, the government owned the rights to research conducted under its grants, but 1980s legislation aimed at commercializing scientific research changed all that, giving government grantees the right to patent and sell their work. Public disgust over Burroughs Wellcome's gouging of AIDS patients with its $10,000 charge for the new drug AZT—developed almost entirely at government expense—soon led to a requirement to charge "reasonable" prices for drugs developed at the NIH itself. But even this requirement, covering perhaps 10 percent of NIH-funded research, was half-heartedly (or perhaps inexpertly) enforced.

Taxol is probably the most disturbing case of this public-private handoff. A major accomplishment in the treatment of breast and ovarian cancer, it was developed by the NIH over two decades. In 1991, the NIH gave Bristol-Myers Squibb the exclusive right to market the drug for five years. According to Love, the National Cancer Institute team then gave Bristol-Myers Squibb an arbitrary list of fifteen cancer drugs and said it expected Taxol to be comparably priced. The lowest-cost drug on the list, levamisole, was only $6 a pill, but it was considered by some to be overpriced because the same drug when used to deworm sheep cost only six *cents* a pill. "NCI was, in essence, telling Bristol-Myers Squibb that it could price Taxol, a government-funded drug invention, the same as other cancer drugs, regardless of where the funding came from, and regardless of how 'fair' those prices were," Love told senators in 1993. A 1998 investigation into the development and pricing of Taxol by the *Washington Post Magazine* suggests that the NCI representatives may have been misled by the price BMS initially announced—not a retail but a direct-from-manufacturer price, and one based on a lower-than-average dose for a very slight (105-pound) woman. The same *Post* investigation reports that in fact, when Taxol was introduced, it became the most expensive cancer drug on the market. A dose of Taxol is listed at about $1,800; a full treatment typically includes numerous injections, with the bill mounting to perhaps $10,000 for ovarian cancer patients, and to $20,000 for breast cancer patients.

Without divulging details of its spending on Taxol, BMS claims it has invested nearly $1 billion in clinical trials to test the drug in a wider array of cancers and to solve thorny manufacturing problems associated with Taxol, which is derived from yew trees. "Taxol has been priced fairly and responsibly in accordance with the reasonable pricing clause," Bristol-Myers Squibb CEO Peter Dolan writes in a letter to employees posted on the company's web site.

Meanwhile, BMS recently settled (without admission of

wrongdoing) claims by twenty-nine state attorneys general that the company violated antitrust laws to extend its monopoly on Taxol by more than three years. In 1993, a BMS executive assured a House committee upset over Taxol's price that the drug wasn't patentable and would face "near-term" generic competition. But BMS proceeded to secure patent protection for Taxol and to sue firms that applied for permission to market generic versions after the government-granted five-year exclusivity period expired. Since that time, according to the National Association of Attorneys General, brand-name Taxol has garnered revenues of at least $5.4 billion for BMS. Although a generic is now available, says Maryland's Andrus, "You figure every month, every week they were able to hold the exclusive market was extremely lucrative. There have been reports that some indigent patients weren't getting the drug because it was just too expensive."

Notwithstanding the toothlessness of the reasonable-pricing language, drug companies were apparently scared off, perhaps because the measure threatened to establish a method for determining fair prices based on a company's real investments. Whatever the case, in 1995 the NIH dumped the reasonable-pricing requirement, and drugmakers began to show more enthusiasm for doing business with America's most prized research institution. NIHCM reports that of 619 formal R&D agreements executed by the NIH between 1993 and 1999, 515 occurred after the reasonable-pricing clause was nixed. Sanders has offered his colleagues in Congress numerous proposals to reinstate the requirement; in 2001, the measure passed in the House but was dropped in conference.

## *THE PROOF OF THE PUDDING: PHARMACEUTICAL PROFITS*

This single fact makes drug industry poor-mouthing about the risk of R&D unconvincing: The drug business is the most profitable in the country and has been at or near the top of the list for decades. While the average Fortune 500 company saw declining profits in a difficult environment in 2001, drug companies on the list actually boosted their profits by 33 percent, according to an analysis of Fortune 500 data by Public Citizen. These titan drugmakers took 18.5 percent of revenues as profit—eight times the median for all other Fortune 500 companies. In other words, whatever the unique exigencies of pharmaceutical R&D, the big drug companies have managed to develop drugs and to sell them at higher profits than are enjoyed by the biggest oil companies, entertainment companies, automakers, and commercial banks.

In response to these much-cited Fortune 500 data, drug-industry reps tend to cite the work of various economists who believe the numbers exaggerate the extent to which pharmaceutical profits dwarf those of other industries. As Princeton University economist Uwe E. Reinhardt, Ph.D., explains, grocery stores can earn relatively handsome returns on their total assets by earning profit margins of only a few pennies per dollar of sales. But unlike grocery stores, drug companies invest heavily in R&D and thus must earn more profit per dollar of sales in order to achieve the same return on their total assets. Put more simply, the profits of pharmaceutical companies should be compared only to those of other capital-intensive industries. But here's the thing: Even after the drug industry's profits are fully "risk-adjusted," no industry appears to have posted more reliable or robust profits. Indeed, that the industry puts down a lot of capital in the ordinary course of business makes it a high-stakes game, but not necessarily "risky" in the sense most of us understand it. Yes, the field is strewn with expensive and ultimately failed R&D projects; but in the aggregate, drugmakers' profitability has been nothing if not consistent. Says Jerome Hoffman, MD, an expert in research methodology and professor of emergency medicine at the University of California, Los Angeles, "It's hard for me to understand how an industry that's the most successful in the world for thirty years, every year, can be the most risky."

With all their wealth, pharmaceutical companies are often good employers and sought-after corporate neighbors that contribute to local cultural and educational programs. As one specialty employment guide tells job seekers, "Pharmaceutical manufacturing is an almost recession proof business, and it remains somewhat insulated from economic cycles that affect other commercial endeavors ... This means job security, promotions, and healthy salaries." A St. Louis, Missouri, opening for a salesperson with a college degree and at least a year of experience seems fairly typical: It offers base pay of $45,000 to $60,000 a year, plus commission, 5,000 shares of stock options, medical and dental coverage, a 401(k), and a company car.

Of course at the top of the corporate ladder, the sums are far more dizzying; the 1990s were especially good to industry executives. The consumer group Families USA recently examined financial filings by nine drugmakers that produce the fifty best-selling drugs for seniors. In 2000, executives in the top slot at each of these companies earned almost $19 million on average. None of the twenty-five highest-paid executives earned less than $5.9 million. And that's not counting stock options. The chairman and CEO of Bristol-Myers Squibb held unexercised options valued at $227.9 million.

In the year 2002, though, the pharmaceutical industry found itself in an unusual period of uncertainty. While some companies continued to grow and thrive, others slogged through a soup of patent expirations, regulatory action, manufacturing glitches, lower earnings, and disappointing research pipelines—all of which sent drug stocks, along with other highfliers of the 1990s, down. It's as if Big Pharma were staggering under its own weight. It remains to be seen where this trend is going. Recently released drug-sales figures for 2002 show a 12 percent increase over 2001 North American sales—a slump most business leaders would consider nothing to cry about.

In the meantime, the weight of Big Pharma is one that Americans have borne and continue to bear disproportionately. Our "free pricing," vast population, and sky's-the-limit demand are what drives drug profits worldwide. But even this basic fact creates occasion for dispute. Whereas many consumer groups and politicians say it's our prices that are out of whack, industry supporters insist that other wealthy consumers—the Europeans and the Japanese, for example—should pay more for drugs and that their refusal to do so, unfair as it is, leaves the responsibility for R&D in American hands. There it is again: Do anything to curtail drug spending in the United States, and you can forget about a cure for Alzheimer's.

Perhaps there's another way to look at it. The drug industry's higher-than-average profits—the pot of gold at the end of the rainbow—has fueled increasing investments in R&D. This means that as in other businesses, the consumer not only pays the cost of making the product but subsidizes the growth of the industry itself. That the drug industry has managed to elevate its development effort to the status of sacred cow (touch it and lives will be lost) obscures a slew of important questions. Have all these R&D dollars been efficiently deployed from a business standpoint, much less from the public's point of view? Does the industry really need to grow at a double-digit clip in order to produce medicines and make money? In the last ten years, R&D spending grew at 14 percent per year, says the economist Reinhardt. This rate of increase, he calculates, gets you to about $500 billion by the year 2025. "The question I raise is well, who's to say that's the right number? And then the pharmaceutical industry says, well, the market." But when buyers try to limit drug spending, drugmakers tend not to accept these efforts as reflecting the wisdom of a free market. Reinhardt observes, "When the market responds, they scream."

The international health-advocacy group Doctors Without Borders (DWB) calls it a "fatal imbalance" that worldwide R&D comes up with fistfuls of drugs to treat, for example, the Western scourge of heart disease—179 drugs over the last twenty-five years—but has offered only 15 new drugs for tropical diseases and tuberculosis, which affect just as many people in poorer nations. "[P]rofit, not need, is driving the development of new medicines," says DWB international council president Morten Rostrup, MD. But if the outcome for the developing world is more stark, nothing guarantees that this profit-driven R&D reflects the public-health priorities even of wealthy Americans. Do we really want to pay for the development of baldness remedies instead of getting more important drugs at lower cost so they could help more people? If we were in charge, would we order Pfizer's rivals to get cracking on something to compete with Viagra (as a number are doing) or with cholesterol-reducing Lipitor (already in a crowded class)? Would we want researchers to pour resources into treatments for heart-burn—a minor problem affecting a lot of people—or focus on cancers that tragically mar the lives of a relative few? And whom would we designate to conduct this lifesaving research? Scientists from major research universities or those in the employ of specialized for-profit companies? Obviously, we don't get to make these calls; we don't even have access to information that would let us lay it all on the table to see where R&D resources are being spent. All we do is sign the checks. Have American consumers, disgruntled about costs but confident our dollars were funding Project Banish Disease, in fact been drafted into Operation Grow Big Pharma? Are we really to believe they're one and the same?

Harvard University economist F. M. Scherer, Ph.D., has described the drug industry's R&D expenditures as "virtuous rent-seeking," meaning that the promise of very rich rewards induces companies to spend outsized sums in order to compete for those rewards; he calls these efforts "virtuous" because drug development has social value. But Scherer supports the notion of universal health care, which would invariably mean government efforts at cost containment and lower profits for drugmakers. "It's true they'd spend less money on research and development," says

Scherer. "The tough question is, how many important new drugs would we lose? And what you would lose on average is products at the margin that probably don't make a difference between life and death."

Here's another point that industry spokespeople tend to overlook when holding up the hundreds of millions spent on R&D: Drug companies receive substantial tax breaks designed precisely to support and encourage that work. In addition, drugmakers have benefited disproportionately during the 1980s and 1990s from a tax provision—slated for cancellation in 2005—that rewards investment in U.S. territories. This provision motivated a major geographical shift in drug manufacturing; by 1990, seventeen of the twenty-one most commonly prescribed medicines in the United States were being produced in Puerto Rico. After taking advantage of its various opportunities for tax relief, the drug industry's effective tax rate during the 1990s averaged 26 percent, versus 33 percent for all major U.S. industries, according to a report by the Congressional Research Service. No major industry enjoyed a lower tax rate.

Finally, while the industry suggests restraint on prices would affect only research on breakthrough drugs, others point to drug-company budget items where there seems to be plenty to spare: profits, yes, but also and more important, marketing. Families USA found that in 2000 and 2001, eight of the nine companies selling the most drugs to American seniors spent more than twice as much on marketing and administration as on R&D. "The pharmaceutical industry's repetitious cry that research and development would be curtailed if drug prices are moderated is extraordinarily misleading," said Ron Pollack, director of Families USA, upon releasing the 2001 report. "If meaningful steps are taken to ameliorate fast-growing drug prices, it is corporate profits, expenditures on marketing, and high executive compensation that are more likely to be affected." Interestingly, the British system for limiting drug spending by its National Health Service (NHS) doesn't address prices at all but enforces a public-health-oriented corporate efficiency by capping profits and strictly limiting the percentage of NHS revenue that drugmakers can funnel back into promotion.

Of course, the United States places no such restraints on drugmakers. Whether their increasing R&D investments pan out or disappoint, they will work assiduously—because they're businesses and not public-health advocates—to recoup those investments and sustain high earnings growth by selling lots of product to American consumers. And they have ways of doing that.

# chapter 4

# BIG PHARMA'S WINNING PITCH

ASKED HOW her employer motivates salespeople, Sandra, a veteran rep for a large pharmaceutical company, answers with a slightly nervous laugh, "Pressure." She's expected to visit perhaps eight doctors a day, filing daily call cards that document those contacts, and she's also expected to meet monthly sales quotas, which may come in the form of dollar amounts for each drug she promotes or, at other times, as a target market share for her territory. "How they actually come up with the quota, we never know," she says. (One colleague suspects it involves a complex operation based on the salesperson's grandmother's age.) Whatever the case, Sandra's numbers are regularly compared to local, regional, and national sales averages. If a formulary for a large HMO in a rep's territory doesn't include one of the company's drugs, the sales rep doesn't get a break on quotas. Conversely, every new indication the FDA approves for a drug will mean an immediate bump in sales quotas. And if the company projects earnings based on a new-drug launch, but the launch is postponed? The company may increase quotas on other drugs to make up the difference. As Sandra puts it, "Their sales have to come from somewhere."

Sometimes you just gotta love America. Only in this land of determinedly free enterprise could the drug industry create a marketing juggernaut so truly awesome in scope. An ever-growing army of drug reps works the territory from the Bronx to Biloxi to Baja, getting face time with prescribing physicians in every corner of medical practice while dropping off doughnuts for their office staff. Meanwhile, their employers sponsor research that puts the best possible spin on their products, influencing medical opinion and practice. Through gorgeous print and TV ads, drug companies attach to prescription medicines the same soft-focus, feel-good fantasies we've come to associate with perfumes or cool cars. They're even stepping into new territory with sexy events like the 2001 Viagra Concert Series, headlined by a 1970s band—Earth, Wind and Fire—sure to revive memories of adolescent passion.

The only trouble is, Melva McCuddy is paying for it. She's paying for it when she buys medicine for cancer and high blood pressure and diabetes and depression. Intensive marketing of prescription drugs drives up costs in two ways. First, it's expensive in itself. Financial filings suggest some drugmakers spend roughly one-fourth to one-third of every sales dollar on marketing. Second, it does what marketing and advertising are designed to do: get more people to buy more product, creating brand recognition and loyalty, in some cases even stimulating "needs" where none existed before.

All of this suggests there may be another problem with

these heavy marketing efforts. Medicine, much more than other areas of human endeavor, rests on the promise of utmost objectivity, the closest possible scrutiny of potential confusions or biases. It's thanks to this ethic that we aren't being bled for every ailment under the sun. And yet it seems a violation of the principle to hand drugmakers a critical role in "informing" physicians (through ads in medical journals, published research, conferences, lectures, and countless face-to-face visits) and the public (primarily via ads and free samples) about the drugs in which these companies have an enormous and undisguised financial stake. Perhaps it is the very pervasiveness of industry influence that has created among medical professionals and patients alike a blind spot, a certain willed naïveté about the effects of this influence. Dismissed as just part of the landscape or allowed to pass for public-health education, drug-company salesmanship skews the delivery of health care toward decidedly commercial aims.

If you are a doctor who writes prescriptions, the drug industry would like a moment of your time. In fact, a casual examination of materials used by contract marketing firms to promote their sales services to drug companies leaves the impression that an American doctor is lucky if he can go to the john without running into some kind of industry promotion. Once they are enhanced with a company's logo, examination room products like table paper, drape sheets, and patient gowns provide "a unique vehicle for marketing . . . inside the physician's office." Logo-imprinted patient-file forms and prescription pads likewise "leverage and enhance your brand's overall marketing plan by bringing your message into the examination room at the point of

prescribing as often as required . . . This week . . . next week
. . . every week of the year." Special drug-sample packaging
has been proven to "change physician behavior, resulting in
up to 31 percent more new prescriptions and 14.7 percent
higher market share." Marketing firms boast of "strong KOL
relationships" (that's "key opinion leaders") and "high-end
representatives, such as Pharm.D.s, to influence thought
leaders." Some marketing firms offer in-house educational
facilities accredited to provide the continuing medical education doctors need to renew their practice licenses. Not to
mention "speaker programs," "live symposia," and "dinner
meetings," all "grounded in physician behavior change
models, adult learning principles, and expert clinical con-
tent that influence physician prescribing behavior." One
company advertises its "professional journal" as a marketing opportunity: "more than 300,000 physician exposures
in hospitals"! Others tout their ability to gather intelligence
and, say, provide incentives such as free samples to prescribing physicians based on their patient populations: "Patient
groups that can be addressed are indigent, elderly, nonpre-
scription drug insurance, etc." Another firm specializes in
"interactive brand promotion" smuggled into educational
software for doctors that includes "treatment simulation."

But these are bells and whistles. The drug industry's main
promotional tool is the old-fashioned salesperson who
spends his or her days calling on physician-customers—and
whose ranks have swelled considerably in the last decade,
from 56,000 in 1990 to almost 88,000 in 2000. That's a 57-
percent increase, versus, according to Sager's analysis, a
roughly 10-percent increase in R&D staff during the same
period. The industry's so-called educational program enjoys

the kind of student-teacher ratio public-school teachers dream about: a drug rep for roughly every eight doctors in America. Many physicians too busy seeing patients to study the medical literature rely on these "detailers" as their first and most accessible source of information on new drugs. And while the nature of their product and extent of their access might seem to distinguish drug reps from other salespeople, that is quite simply an illusion. "Commission: 13K at quota, uncapped!" trumpets the aforementioned job posting for a St. Louis rep. The specialty job guide includes a list of sample interview questions with such items as, "What do you think is most important: the Opening Line or a Closing Line? Why?" Subject to the same pressures as salespeople everywhere, Sandra's work is also structured around a similar incentive: a bonus based on sales performance.

"This isn't breakfast cereal," complains Bob Goodman, MD, an internist at New York City's Columbia Presbyterian Medical Center and founder of the web site www.nofreelunch .org, which encourages doctors to resist drug-industry pitches. "You want the drug that works best. But drug reps don't get paid if doctors are prescribing the correct medication, they get paid if doctors are prescribing their medication."

When addressing physician audiences on the subject of industry promotions, UCLA's Hoffman can count on getting a laugh from this one-liner: "Who here has seen an ugly drug rep?" Like all good jokes, it's funny because it reveals a basic truth: The relationship between drug reps and physicians is subject to all the usual rules of human interaction, including the human tendency to be charmed by someone who's attractive, personable, smart, and who aims to please. While drug reps talk for a few minutes about new drugs, they also try to spread a little "goodwill," as Hoffman puts it. "They go out of their way," he says. "They do things that make [doctors] feel good and make their lives a little tiny bit easier."

One busy three-physician general practice in rural Iowa gets visits from drug reps every day. "Today we had three or four," says Jan, an office nurse. "Some days we have ten come in and we've got them out in the waiting room." Often, they bring baked goods from Des Moines that you can't get in town or call ahead to take orders for lunch. Sometimes they offer the doctors tickets to popular University of Iowa games. "They're always dumping pens and sticky pads over the counter at us," says Jan. "It's like a competition to see who's going to come up with the neatest design of pen, one that lights up or does weird stuff." When there's an opening, they chat up the doctors. One regular likes to engage one of the doctors in discussion about their mutual hobby, running. "She follows her around like a puppy," says Jan.

You'll find drug reps just about any place doctors gather. Hospitals. Medical schools. Conferences. "They'll stand next to the table of food and as the people file out to fill their plates with moo-shu pork or whatever, they'll hand out a pen and a coffee mug, and try to talk about their drugs or just offer a friendly face," says Michael Steinman, MD, an internist at the San Francisco Veterans Affairs Medical Center who has studied industry-physician relations.

Maybe you're wondering how your doctor, who has a scant fifteen minutes for you, finds time to engage so many drug reps. Actually, that's a problem. According to *Med Ad News*, the average time physicians spent with drug reps each day dwindled from twelve minutes in 1995 to seven minutes in 2000. With salespeople promoting the same drugs for months, often the docs have already heard what they have to say. Facing this headwind in the competition for "face time" and "share of voice," companies have responded by hiring more reps. "The drug company knows if the Lipitor rep isn't there, the Zocor rep will be," says Ehrlich, CEO of Rx Insight. "It's like a nuclear arms race. We all have enough missiles to destroy the world, but we keep building more."

One large physician group in Cincinnati has a new policy for dealing with sales reps who waylay docs in the corridors: Charge them $65 for ten minutes of undivided attention. The doctors, says Queen City Physicians director of operations Kim Jones, have one of the lowest reimbursement rates in the country. "They have to see as many patients as they can," says Jones. Proceeds from the program are being socked away for an electronic medical-records system, but after a year there isn't much of it. The big companies have, not surprisingly, refused to play. Meanwhile, life is getting tougher for their detailers. "I think the hardest part of our job is that access to physicians has gotten harder," says Sandra. "They're just getting bombarded. If you don't bring them something of value, then why should they waste their time? Why should they take five minutes?" By July, many of the docs on her call list were booked for lunch through November—not that, having carefully studied the clinical research on her products, she looks forward to slinging victuals. "There is nothing worse than going and picking up thirty lunches, lugging heavy gallons of iced tea in the hot sun, only to have a nurse walk in and say, 'I just had that for dinner last night,'" says Sandra.

Indeed, the increasing access problem seems only to have stimulated drug-company ingenuity in finding enticements—besides cash—to win doctors' attention. In much the same way drinks are said to get a party going, gifts are the social lubricant that enables relationships between drug-firm representatives and doctors. On the first day of medical school, students might receive a book, a white jacket, perhaps a stethoscope. "Those first gifts are always educational or useful. What they create right from the start is goodwill and a sense of entitlement," says Hoffman. Later there are any number of small, inexpensive gifts. Then, maybe tickets to sporting events or concerts. Doctors may be invited to come pick up an Easter ham or Valentine's Day flowers or a carryout meal. Or they'll get invitations to fancier dinners: "You'll get mailings to your home: 'Pfizer is sponsoring a midnight cruise on San Francisco Bay with the great chefs of the world and a short talk on the management of arrhythmia!'" says Steinman.

At the grander end of the continuum, drug companies pay for doctors to attend ostensibly educational events that happen to take place at lavish resorts. "Opinion leaders" may get a speaker's fee or be compensated for less-than-grueling consultancy sessions. "I've gone on a couple of junkets myself," admits Gerstein, who as both a physician and HMO executive had significant influence on prescribing. On the second trip, he says, a drug company flew him to San Diego for golf rounds and assorted fun. "They took the entire conference to the San Diego Zoo, and that was an obscene display of luxury in terms of food and liquor and everything else. I just said to myself, 'What the hell am I doing? I'm fighting to keep down the cost of drugs and this is sending them sky-high!" The invitations keep coming, but he turns them down.

Like drug-rep hires, industry sponsorship of educational events has picked up considerably over the last decade. The industry paid for 314,000 such events in 2000, more than four times the 70,000 events held in 1993. In a recent survey of Maryland physicians, about 8 percent reported having given lectures for a drug company. Their colleagues in the audience take in food and wine—as well as a drug-company-sponsored message from speakers invariably chosen for views favorable to the firm.

Some educational events sponsored by the industry provide doctors with the continuing medical education (CME) credits they need to keep up their licenses. These have to be approved by an official accrediting body, and sponsorship often takes the form of general grants. Still, there's concern that industry support leads to bias in the CME curriculum. This worry is especially piqued by the increasing number of for-profit "medical-education" and public-relations firms that have stepped into the multibillion-dollar-a-year CME business. "What often happens is that these third-party commercial education groups put together the program and then go to an academic program and say, 'We've dotted all the i's and crossed the t's, would you be willing to give it the CME credit?" explains Frank Davidoff, MD, former editor of the *Annals of Internal Medicine* and a one-time organizer of CME programs. "There are all these very intimate relationship between industry, third parties, and academic accredited centers to put these things on."

What do doctors think about all these arrangements? A recent survey of first- and second-year residents in one residency program suggests that few are troubled by the sort of crisis of conscience Gerstein describes. A substantial majority found promotions in the form of antibiotic guides, journal article reprints, conference lunches, dinner lectures, pens, social outings, and textbooks to be appropriate. Nearly half the residents thought it was appropriate for drug companies to pay travel expenses to continuing education conferences. Even gifts of luggage were deemed appropriate by a few residents. Interestingly, though, many residents who thought certain promotions were inappropriate had participated in them anyway. All had eaten lunch on the drug companies and accepted their pens, whether they thought it was okay or not. And half the residents who didn't approve of drug-company-sponsored recreational events had taken part in them or planned to do so.

The reason for this seemingly contradictory behavior probably has less to do with the doctors' hypocrisy than with their susceptibility to an attractive but basically flawed supposition: that they're immune from influence. Steinman, who authored the study, comments, "Some people think, 'Maybe other doctors are influenced but I myself am impervious. My colleagues I'm not so sure about, but me, I'm sure about.'" A majority of residents claimed industry promotional activities have "no influence" on their prescribing practices; but only 16 percent said the same for their colleagues. Meanwhile, the doctors reported having received limited education on the ethics of industry-physician relations—over one-third had received none whatsoever—while watching colleagues and mentors accept various industry gifts, lending them "an implicit seal of approval," Steinman wrote.

There's plenty of reason to believe that doctors are not immune from drug-industry pitches. A review of the medical literature on industry-physician contact, published in the *Journal of the American Medical Association (JAMA)* in 2000, found that physician interaction with drug reps was associated with higher prescription costs, "nonrational" prescribing, rapid adoption of new drugs, and decreased prescription of generics. Doctors who had eaten company-sponsored meals were more likely to request that particular drugs be added to their practice formularies. The review reported that when a company sponsored a program to provide doctors' continuing education, the sponsor's drug was "always preferentially highlighted" in the curriculum, and afterward, attendees tended to prescribe the sponsor's drug more often.

Moreover, in a major position paper on industry-physician relations, the American College of Physicians points to a body of social-science literature describing, in culture after culture, the sense of social obligation created by the "gift relationship." "[T]he prevailing purpose of the gift is to establish the identity of the donor in the mind of the recipient and to oblige the recipient to reciprocate," the college counsels members. "The acceptance of even small gifts can affect clinical judgment and heighten the perception (as well as the reality) of a conflict of interest."

Ultimately, it's a matter of common sense: If all these meals and lectures and gifts had no effect, then what possible motive could the drug companies have for providing them? "They definitely work—that's why industry does it," says Goodman.

With this in mind, doctors like Steinman, Hoffman, and

Goodman (and the hundreds of doctors who've joined Goodman in his informal organization, No Free Lunch) refuse all invitations and gifts from the drug industry. Goodman's web site takes a light approach to persuading other doctors to do the same, as in this takeoff on a drug-company ad: "Take the CAGE: Have you ever prescribed **C**elebrex? Do you get **A**nnoyed by people who complain about drug lunches & free gifts? Is there a medication lo**G**o on the pen you're using right now? Do you drink your morning **E**ye-opener out of a Lipitor coffee mug? If you answered YES to 2 or more of the above, you may be drug company dependent. Don't despair. There may be HELP!" The site is also full of information, including advice on how to assess the validity of research touted by drug-company ads in medical journals. "My message is really intended for physicians," says Goodman. "What industries do is market their products—but that's not what physicians are supposed to be doing."

Indeed, in response to heightened public scrutiny of its marketing practices, the industry itself has issued voluntary guidelines discouraging purely social or recreational perks for doctors. PhRMA's code, launched in July 2002, explicitly discourages companies from giving gifts—such as gasoline, take-out food, flowers, and concert tickets—that clearly have nothing to do with patient care. Neither is it permissible under the code to pay for attendees' travel and honoraria to educational meetings (although paying speakers' and consultants' expenses and fees is deemed legitimate). Goodman and others think it may curtail the more colorful excesses of the industry-doctor "gift relationship." Sandra says her company is taking the code "very seriously."

On the other hand, a voluntary code adopted in 1990 by the American Medical Association has been widely flouted; it recommends that doctors accept only gifts of modest value and that serve some educational or patient-care purpose. Moreover, PhRMA's insistence in the new code's preamble that industry interaction with docs is designed with no other intent than "to benefit patients and to enhance the practice of medicine" seems to be another refusal to identify salesmanship for what it is. In some cases, the PhRMA code is striking for what it *does* sanction. For example, it's judged appropriate for a company to invite 300 physicians for two days of training to prepare them to speak on behalf of the company. An event of this sort could take place at a regional resort, with trainees paid for their time, expenses, and "a few hours of golf." For the most part, of course, the doctors would be busy getting "educated by a faculty on the full range of data surrounding the disease state and the Company's drug product ... ."

Neither does the code address the most valuable industry "gift" to doctors, the very bulwark of its promotional campaign: free drug samples. Over the course of a year, during all those visits to hospitals and doctors' offices, drug reps hand out millions of doses of their products. The total retail value of these free samples is almost $8 billion—half the industry's overall promotional spending. "I can't even imagine what we go through every year in free medicine," says Jan, the Iowa nurse.

Drug sampling is different from, say, the distribution of Easter hams, in that doctors and patients tend to see it as enhancing patient care. In one study, 86 percent of physicians said they support sampling. In turn, many patients who struggle to pay their prescription bills express gratitude toward their doctors for giving them samples. On the surface at least, everyone wins. The drug company increases awareness of its new drug. The doctor endears himself to patients by offering them something of real value. (Indeed, a generally positive feeling may spread through the doctor's office, as, according to one study, one-third of samples are used by the physicians themselves, their families, and staff.) And the patient can test out a new drug—which, after all, may or may not work well—without incurring any expense or even going to the pharmacy.

What's the catch? "Samples are always the newest and most expensive medication," says Goodman. "The doctor gives the patient a few samples, the patient likes them, that's what he wants, and the next time he gets a prescription for Vioxx or Celebrex rather than for generic ibuprofen, which would have been just as good for the patient. It's really a very powerful promotional tool." Sampling effectively lowers the threshold for prescribing and taking a costly new drug. At the critical moment—the "point-of-decision," to quote the marketers' jargon—the drug is there, and it's free. Once the patient's on it, he or she is more likely to stay on it. And the doctor, now familiar with the drug, may be likely to prescribe it to others.

Ironically, the astronomical cost of new drugs is part of what makes the free samples so sought-after. Jan takes home Plavix for her grandfather, who'd otherwise have to make a $60 monthly co-pay for the blood-thinning drug. Plavix prescriptions rose 37 percent last year. For her husband, she brings home the new bladder-control medicine Detrol LA, which has an average prescription cost of about

$86. Both drugs were among the top fifty contributors to last year's increase in drug spending. But as Jan knows better than most, when the company stops promoting the drugs, the samples may run dry; over the past twelve months or so, local reps stopped sampling a headache medication, an oral contraceptive, and a thyroid-hormone replacement medicine. Although she and her coworkers try hard to keep patients in free medicine, Jan says, "They assume that we have samples all the time and that we know when they're going to be there—and we have no clue."

Darcy Landy, fifty-six, a former RN in Maine who suffers from bipolar disorder, says her psychiatrist warned her that the makers of her expensive antidepressant, anti-anxiety, and antipsychotic medications might stop sampling them. "It scared me, and then when it finally happened it scared me more," says Landy. "I need to have this medicine to live." This combo of medicines works better than anything she's tried in the past. Worried that any changes could land her in the hospital—it's happened before—she scrapes together the $4,100 a year, saving hundreds by making trips to Canada.

The question for doctors, patients, and the insurers who pay the bills is whether a cheaper drug would work just as well as the new brand-name that happens to be in the doctor's sample cabinet. What if the drug that was free and readily at hand were a generic? Insurer Highmark Blue Cross Blue Shield and its PBM Merck-Medco recently launched a program to offer doctors generics samples, with impressive results. Among the 1,700 physicians nationwide who received visits from a clinical pharmacist and access to the free samples, there was a 22-percent increase in generic prescribing within eighteen months of the program's launch.

"Generics First proves you can manage drug trends in a way that maintains or improves physician and patient satisfaction," Merck-Medco's chief medical officer Robert Epstein, MD, said in announcing the results. "Moreover, it proves samples matter."

## SPINNING SCIENCE: THE COMMERCIALIZATION OF CLINICAL TRIALS

Doctors determined not to rely on industry representations about their products will—like generations of physicians subject to the various cultural, political, and economic pressures of their times—seek out the results of research conducted according to the strictures of science. In clinical trials, the safety and effectiveness of drugs are systematically tested in real people. These clinical trials, published and reviewed in widely respected medical journals, and taken together, form the basis of accepted medical practice. What works. What works better. Which drugs are likely to produce side effects A and B in certain patients.

The drug industry pays for the majority of this research. Fully 70 percent of funds to support U.S. drug trials come from drug companies, according to an article in the *New England Journal of Medicine* by Thomas Bodenheimer, MD, a longtime practicing doctor and health-care policy researcher. Indeed, companies are required to perform the studies in order to gain FDA approval for their products or to support any product claims they might wish to make after approval. Bodenheimer and others are quick to point out that many of these trials meet the highest standards for scientific inquiry. With that broad caveat in mind, the process is full of opportunities for drug companies to mold the message that emerges from research.

As Bodenheimer's *New England Journal* piece documents, the 1990s have seen a dramatic change in the way industry-sponsored trials are conducted—a shift that gives drug companies more control over how studies are designed, how the resulting data are organized and presented, and whether these data are made public at all. In some cases, drug companies have bent research to their own purposes, making it not the gold standard for objectivity practicing physicians expect, but, by virtue of this expectation, the ultimate marketing tool.

In the past, the vast majority of drug trials, including those sponsored by industry, were performed in university hospitals by academic researchers. In 1991, 80 percent of drug-industry money for trials went to academic medical centers. By 1998, the majority of these funds had been handed instead to a new animal on the research scene: the contract research organization (CRO). CROs are for-profit companies that pull together the various aspects of a clinical trial in much the way producers make movies. This may include designing the study, setting up a network of research sites in hospitals and doctor's offices, supervising the collection of data, analyzing those data, and, finally, preparing applications for FDA approval and manuscripts for publication. They do all this more quickly and cheaply than universities do. These entrepreneurial operations also provide their clients—the drug companies—with an unprecedented level of control over the entire process.

It is testimony to the commercial orientation of CROs

that a few have formed business alliances with some of the world's biggest advertising agencies; together they help drugmaker-clients translate research into sales. "The disciplines of clinical drug development and strategic drug commercialization are converging at an astonishingly fast pace," an executive of Omnicom Group Inc., a global marketing company, said in a statement announcing the firm's 1999 investment in a CRO called Scirex. "With the goal today being faster, smarter and more efficient commercialization of new drugs," he said, "we felt that we needed to be closer to the test tube—to actually work with clinical scientists to develop drugs."

Meanwhile, partly as a result of competition from CROs, academic medical centers are themselves allowing more aggressive incursions by industry sponsors into the conduct of their research. "Arm's-length relationships are a thing of the past, and financial arrangements are hardly limited to grant support," Marcia Angell, MD, former editor of the *New England Journal of Medicine*, told colleagues at a conference on conflicts of interest in research. Companies increasingly insist on designing studies and controlling the raw data; some investigators may not even be allowed to see all the numbers. If results are unfavorable, drugmakers are sometimes able to prevent them from coming to light—despite partnerships with academic researchers for whom publication is a professional priority. In a survey of university-industry research centers published in 1994, Carnegie-Mellon University found that 35 percent of signed agreements allowed the sponsor to delete information from publication; 53 percent allowed publication to be delayed; and 30 percent allowed both. During late 2001 and early

2002, Duke University researchers interviewed officials at 108 U.S. medical schools and found that guidelines for agreements between industry sponsors and researchers, issued by the International Committee of Medical Journal Editors, are largely ignored. Only 1 percent of the agreements guaranteed that authors of reports on multisite studies would have access to all the trial data.

Increasingly, researchers themselves have financial stakes in the drugs they're testing, as company consultants, as speakers, or more directly, as stockholders in the companies that make the drugs. In a 2000 *New England Journal* piece, "Is Academic Medicine for Sale?" Angell noted that her own university, Harvard, had unusually stringent guidelines that nonetheless allowed researchers to own up to $20,000 worth of stock in the company whose drug was under study. Angell and other medical-journal editors have reported that when seeking contributors to write review articles, they've often been hard-pressed to find expert researchers who are free of ties to the companies that dominate their fields.

These conflicts of interest raise concern for the human subjects on whom drugs are being tested. Are they fully informed about the relationship? Are they being exposed to undue risk or being retained in the study inappropriately? In a much-publicized 1999 case, a healthy teenager suffered a fatal reaction to a gene therapy drug being tested at the University of Pennsylvania by a research scientist who owned a large stake in the company propounding the therapy; when the company was sold, the scientist reportedly made millions. And in 2001, the *Seattle Times* reported that patients had died unnecessarily while receiving experimental cancer treatments at the renowned Fred Hutchinson Cancer Research Center. The *Seattle Times* claimed patients weren't told the physician-investigators were also among the first stockholders in the biotech start-up that owned the test drug.

A less worrying but more widespread conflict of interest is evident in the office-based doctor who receives a fee for every patient he or she enrolls in a drug-industry trial. "When most research was done in academic medical centers, it was largely the case that the investigator was not your personal physician," explains Lois Snyder, J.D., director of the Center for Ethics and Professionalism of the American College of Physicians. Patients recruited by their own physicians may be more inclined to simply follow the doc's advice without being aware that their physician is "acting in two different roles," says Snyder. In the Maryland study already cited, one in ten doctors surveyed had run clinical trials for a drug company.

In fact, some drug-industry studies, known as "seeding trials," have every appearance of being nothing more than campaigns to convince investigator-doctors and their patients to use the drug in question. In a 1994 article in the *New England Journal of Medicine*, then FDA head David Kessler, MD, explained that such trials are distinguished by their apparent lack of intention to find out anything about the drug. Kessler cited one example in which a company's sales force recruited 2,500 office-based doctors and paid them $1,050 each to enroll twelve patients in a "study" of its new blood-pressure medicine, which was entering a field crowded with similar products. There was no control group. In another case, Kessler quotes from a memo a drug-company's marketing department sent to sales reps: "Make no mistake about it:

The [name of drug omitted] study is the single most important sales initiative of 1993 ... If at least 20,000 of the 25,000 patients involved in the study remain on [the drug], it could mean up to a $10,000,000 boost in sales. In Phase II, this figure could double."

To enroll patients in a "trial" that lacks even a shred of scientific worth clearly isn't right. But it also seems fair to ask whether it's ethical to enlist human subjects in the production of findings that although scientifically valid, are useful mainly to support marketing claims. Virginia Sharpe, Ph.D., director of the Integrity in Science Project of the Center for Science in the Public Interest, puts it this way: "If the research is being conducted to produce drugs or devices that will have only a marginal benefit, will have only a cosmetic benefit, or will have no benefit over the drugs or devices that are currently on the market, is it justifiable?"

Of course, once the trials are wrapped and the data analyzed, the results may affect many more patients by influencing medical opinion and practice. And subtle manipulations of design and analysis are likely to escape the notice of all but the most sophisticated. Sponsor companies might tip the balance in their favor by using their drug at higher doses than a comparison drug. This was the case, according to a 1994 study, in over half of industry-sponsored trials of non-steroidal anti-inflammatory drugs (NSAIDs) to treat arthritis. Or the drug can be studied in populations that are healthier than those in which it's likely to be used. Companies might also use a shorter timeline than is necessary to study the drug's full effects. The *Washington Post* reported last year on an influential yearlong study of gastrointestinal side effects run by the makers of the arthritis medication

Celebrex. Pharmacia was able to report favorably on its product, but only by dropping out six months' worth of data. Another way to fudge: Collect data on a number of "end points"—you might be looking for symptom relief, or blood-test results, or incidence of adverse events like heart attacks—and report only those end points that present the drug in a good light.

"You're doing this research, sponsorship comes from the company, and—I don't think it's conscious—you're looking for something good about the drug," says Hoffman. "Even if that something good is irrelevant and is balanced by something bad. You can interpret almost any project in a way that looks favorable."

If the numbers don't prove malleable, then the words that accompany them might. Davidoff recounts how, as editor of *Annals of Internal Medicine,* he and his colleagues noticed that in the narrative describing their work, one group of researchers had reported far more positively on a drug's effects than seemed justified by the data they presented. He spoke to the author, who resubmitted the report, still with the same language. It finally emerged that the company sponsoring the research had reserved the right to review—and, apparently, to edit—the manuscript (which was eventually published with a conflict-of-interest disclosure).

Indeed, another way to subtly alter the effect of a published study is to obfuscate about where the work is "coming from," literally and figuratively. Journal editors, Davidoff says, are increasingly aware of various methods for doing this, informally known as the three Gs. "Ghosts," he says, are people who did the work but aren't credited because of their association with a sponsor company or because they had less influence in the group. "Gifts" refers to the practice of crediting an influential researcher, perhaps the laboratory's director, who did little work on the study at hand but whose name might bring prestige and increase the likelihood of publication. Perhaps most disturbingly, "guests" are simply invited by a drug company to review a finished paper and put their name to it, for a fee. "It's not everyday," says Davidoff, "but it's not rare either."

In an infamous case of behind-the-scenes strong-arming, Boots Pharmaceuticals won numerous changes to a 1994 manuscript by researcher Betty Dong, Pharm.D., but still wasn't satisfied. The market dominance of Boots's Synthroid, a thyroid-hormone replacement drug, rested on claims that it worked better than cheaper versions of the hormone. But Dong's work comparing Synthroid with three other drugs found them to be equivalent. After the study had been accepted by *JAMA*, Boots threatened to sue Dong under a contract that gave Boots the right to withhold publication, one of Dong's collaborators told the *Wall Street Journal* in 1996. Although a Boots executive denied making the threat, Dong soon wrote *JAMA* to withdraw the paper, citing impending legal action. Boots published her data, with a contradictory spin, in another publication. By the time *JAMA* finally published Dong's study seven years after its completion, Boots—largely on the strength of top-selling Synthroid—had been acquired for $1.4 billion.

Moreover, in publishing Dong's work, *JAMA* editor Drummond Rennie, MD, noted that he'd had to search far and wide for thyroid experts to review the paper who were free of financial ties to what was now Boots/Knoll. Rennie further commented that the American Thyroid Association, a professional group that had narrowly voted against writing to Knoll to request publication of Dong's study, relied on the company for more than 60 percent of its commercial funding.

The bottom line shouldn't be surprising: Company-sponsored trials that do get published tend to say good things, and not bad things, about the drugs in question. One 1996 study published in the *Annals of Internal Medicine* reviewed company-supported drug studies published between 1980 and 1989 in peer-reviewed journals or symposia proceedings and found that nearly all of them—98 percent—favored the company's drug.

# [chapter 5]

## GETTING TO YOU

DRUGMAKERS' EFFORTS to influence doctors' behavior are ultimately aimed at influencing ours. And more than ever before, these companies are bringing their pitch straight into Americans' everyday lives, advertising on radio, in popular magazines, and especially on TV. Here the message eschews the dry language of clinical research, its end points and data sets, for the powerful emotional image: a flower opening, an old person frolicking like a colt, people of all colors linking arms. Or to strike a different mood, an apparently healthy middle-aged woman suddenly dropping from the frame.

Although magazine ads weren't uncommon in the 1980s, direct-to-consumer (DTC) drug advertising is largely a phenomenon that arose in the 1990s. A 1997 FDA rule making it more practical to advertise on television—companies could now substitute a toll-free number or web address for the "small print" details about drug side effects and contraindications—was undoubtedly an important catalyst. Then a few bold and enormously successful campaigns convinced other big players that they couldn't afford to stay on the sidelines. Spending on consumer ads surged from a scant $266 million in 1994 to $2.6 billion in 2001. Controversial in the United States, the practice of pushing prescription medicine much the same way as soda pop is virtually unheard of elsewhere in the developed world. As Boston University's Sager says, "They're laughing at us again."

Traditionally, prescription drugmakers have emphasized as a defining feature of their industry that they did not advertise to the consumer, but only to the learned physician. Among other things, this approach facilitated the industry's close association with scientific authority. The recent promotional focus on patients reflects a sea change in medicine and in culture itself. As Mickey Smith, Ph.D., an expert in pharmaceutical marketing at the University of Mississippi, puts it, "People are much better educated—not smarter necessarily, but better educated. The ads you see right now, if they'd run in the Fifties, would have fallen on deaf ears because people wouldn't have had a clue what you were talking about." Now that you, Consumer, are trawling the Internet for health information, now that you're motivated to take care of yourself and empowered to make decisions about your own medical care, the drug industry would like a moment of your time.

The ads seem to be getting the job done, reaching the great majority of Americans, winning their trust, and, in more than a few cases, prompting people to ask for a drug by name. Nine out of ten consumers surveyed in 2000 by *Prevention Magazine* said they'd seen or heard a drug ad. When queried by the Henry J. Kaiser Family Foundation in 2001,

30 percent of consumers reported having talked with their doctor about a drug they'd seen advertised. Nearly half of those who asked for an advertised drug—13 percent of all consumers—came away with a script. In another Kaiser study, co-sponsored by *The NewsHour with Jim Lehrer*, nearly half of American consumers said they trust advertisements to provide them with accurate information. But perhaps most telling are these results of a recent NIHCM study: Between 1999 and 2000, prescriptions for the fifty most heavily advertised drugs rose at six times the rate of all other drugs. Sales of those fifty intensively promoted drugs were responsible for almost half the increase in Americans' overall drug spending that year. Makers of the new arthritis drug Vioxx spent $160 million pushing it to consumers in 2000, more advertising dollars than were dropped on Pepsi Cola, Budweiser beer, Nike shoes, or Campbell's soups. Vioxx sales shot up 360 percent.

The way industry spokespeople tell it, Americans should count themselves lucky—drug ads are educational, informing us about health conditions so we can seek appropriate treatment. "The bottom line is that direct-to-consumer advertising is good for patients and good for public health," says a PhRMA spokesman. Sometimes public-health goals do overlap with marketing goals: More people recognizing the signs of clinical depression might boost antidepressant sales and bring relief to many. But skeptics of the drug industry's ads-equal-education equation point out that plenty of important public-health messages go begging for want of profit potential. For example, several pharmaceutical companies have introduced discount programs for low-income seniors. "Have you seen one ad promoting those discount cards?" asks Wennar, of United Health Alliance in Vermont. "Do they do anything on TV to tell people about them?"

What we're getting from DTC drug advertising is lots of exposure to a relatively small number of drugs—generally speaking, new medicines with huge markets and plenty of patent life left. The Kaiser Family Foundation reports that with thousands of drugs on the market, 60 percent of DTC spending in 2000 went to plug just twenty products. This intensive exposure creates what ad people call "brand awareness." A recent survey by market research firm Insight-Express found that, for example, 74 percent of respondents knew Claritin by name. More than half recognized Paxil, 45 percent knew the cholesterol-lowering Zocor, and nearly 80 percent were aware of the pharmaceutical phenomenon Viagra. All have been among the most heavily advertised drug products.

As for what else people take away from the ads, opinions are mixed, and consumer research is limited. One AARP survey found that one-third of the DTC audience failed to notice fine-print information on indications, side effects, and other issues included in magazine ads. Of those who did notice the information, two-thirds said they weren't in the habit of reading it. TV ads have to direct consumers to a phone number, web site, or other ad where they can get more information. But in a Kaiser Family Foundation study, nine out of ten respondents shown three televised drug ads couldn't remember where to get this additional information. Respondents who were shown the drug ads (which included mention of major side effects) judged the side effects to be more serious than those who hadn't seen the ads, but just after viewing the ad, only about half could identify the side effects.

As in all advertising, the main event isn't the discursive information the ads deliver directly, but the suggestive fantasies buried in their music and pictures. "The Nexium ads are so phenomenal that I'd like to take the drug and I don't even have the problem," says Gerstein. "They show a variety of people, very diverse, all standing on jagged stone promontories, and they all start moving together . . . If Disney had done it, you'd say 'Wonderful!'" An ad for an oral contraceptive shows a couple grinning and nuzzling, with the tag line, "Isn't it great when you finally find the right one?" The sound track is a tune whose words—not heard in the ad—are, "This will be an everlasting love."

Other drug ads trade on the cachet of various famous people—baseball legend Cal Ripken Jr., pitching a blood-pressure drug, figure skater Dorothy Hamill praising arthritis medicine, journalist Joan Lunden flogging an allergy med. *Med Ad News* recently reported on a team-up between pharmaceutical-marketing firm Catalyst Communications and a sports-marketing company founded by a former New York Yankees VP. Catalyst's chief stated, "We chose Perello & Company because it understands the divergent worlds of pharmaceuticals and sports." So much for the square in the white coat. Indeed, the use of celebrities has facilitated the industry's bringing together any number of divergent worlds. Is it journalism or is it advertising? Is it fantasy or real life?

Naturally reporters' and editors' in-boxes are stuffed with company press releases and ready-made copy—perhaps a feature on a golf pro's arthritis and how he overcame it with

Drug X. That's par for the course. What's surprising and not a little disturbing is that some big stars have been getting air on major news outlets to chat about their conditions and urge others to seek treatment—without anyone mentioning they were being paid by a drug company. Newspeople were chagrined by a *New York Times* exposé in the summer of 2002 that depicted a veritable three-ring circus: Kathleen Turner raving to *Good Morning America*'s Diane Sawyer about "extraordinarily effective" new medications to treat her rheumatoid arthritis (thank you, Wyeth); Lauren Bacall spooking the daylights out of *Today* viewers over an eye disease that can cause blindness (thank you, Novartis); actor Noah Wyle being interviewed as if he were an expert in post-traumatic stress disorder, even as his fictional character on *ER* endured the aftermath of a violent attack (thanks, Pfizer). A week after the *Times* report, CNN did a story telling viewers that some celebrities interviewed on its own network had been paid by drug companies. It announced a new policy of asking famous people scheduled to talk about medical issues whether they have financial ties to related companies and to reveal any such ties on the air.

As long as they don't mention a drug by name, celebs stirring up interest in a particular disease don't have to adhere to the FDA's "fair balance" rule, which requires that any claim linking a specific drug to a specific action be accompanied by mention of the drug's limitations and side effects. Ads can accomplish this, too. "Reminder" ads feature the name of a drug without saying what it's for; they may have the stylized vagueness of ads for hip perfumes. Other drug ads come off as public-service announcements: Bob Dole wants to talk to you about erectile dysfunction. These "help-seeking" ads mention a condition and may flash the company name, but won't name the drug (Viagra) you'll get when you follow the ad's exhortation to see your doctor.

Indeed, to browse the archives of FDA notices of violation to drug companies for misleading ads is to get a sense of how utterly at a loss the agency is to address the various ways expert image makers get across their "claims." Here's what the FDA had to say about an ad for the sleep aid Ambien: "The reminder advertisement presents graphics of the sun and the earth going from night to day, a flower closing and opening, and the Ambien tablet falling on a sheet or pillow, together with the verbal statement 'the rhythm of life.' Thus, the advertisement in total, with the graphics and verbal statement, makes a representation about the product." "Reminder" ads—which don't have to name side effects—aren't supposed to make claims either. But *every* ad makes a representation about a product. What else is an ad for?

Another FDA notice complained that the "totality of the images, the music, and the audio statements" in a sixty-second TV spot for arthritis med Celebrex overstated the drug's efficacy. The ad showed silver-haired arthritis sufferers rowing boats and riding scooters to the joyous sound track, "Celebrate, celebrate, do what you like to do!" (Celebrex hasn't been shown to reduce pain any more effectively than, for example, the generic ibuprofen that sells for a fraction of the cost.) The Celebrex spots have changed—most ads cited by the FDA are either modified or pulled without further regulatory action—but they communicate the same basic idea, with an attractive, well-dressed older couple dancing energetically to happy music. You could argue that the ads associate Celebrex not only with pain relief (whether exaggerated or not is subjective) but also with energy, wealth, youth, beauty, and a happy marriage. That's how the medium works. As one professor of pharmacy puts it, "They're making it look chic to take certain drugs. You don't focus on the product or the disease, you focus on the lifestyle that the drug allows or creates. They're selling lifestyles, not drugs."

Still another FDA missive ordered the discontinuation of a consumer mailer that touted brand-name tamoxifen (Nolvadex) for prevention of breast cancer in women at high risk for the disease. The agency said the mailer overstated the drug's efficacy in this role, minimized side effects, and failed to make clear that women who score 1.7 on a breast-cancer risk assessment, though they may be considered "high risk," have only a 1.7 percent chance of getting breast cancer. But FDA enforcers didn't mention—and in fact are not empowered to address—how the brochure, titled "Are You a Helpless Female?" capitalized on women's terror, with models who stare fixedly at the reader and the tag line: "Now *predict* your chances of getting *breast cancer*. And *act* on it."

Even a drug's trade name is an advertisement, enlisting the deep and not always conscious associations of language to tout the drug's wonderful qualities wherever and whenever it's mentioned. Hardly indifferent to this fact, drugmakers put a good deal of effort into inventing brand names, sometimes hiring outside consultants to conduct market research and screen the name for unfortunate connotations in an array of languages. Sildenafil is one thing—but Viagra, with its suggestion of vitality, virility, and the mighty flow of the Niagara, is quite another. According to one report, Lilly's new impotence drug Cialis was derived from the French word for sky, *ciel,* to give users the impression that "the sky's the limit." The alchemy of naming turns the rather awkward atorvastatin into Lipitor, which combines the word for blood fats, "lipid," with a hint of the avenging action hero. And Baycol (a cholesterol reducer withdrawn from the market for safety reasons)—can it be a coincidence that the name invokes a certain tasty (if fatty) breakfast meat?

The fact is, it's not the job of advertising (or "branding," as marketers call it) to educate, to put it all in context. In the Kaiser study, respondents who'd seen an ad for Nexium were more likely to know that heartburn and acid reflux can lead to more serious stomach problems—but did they understand that more often than not, this doesn't happen? And did the ad give them insight into whether this problem affects them personally? It's extremely rare for an ad to give information about a drug's mechanism of action, success rate, or length of treatment, much less about alternative treatments or cost. "Let's pretend that a drug ad is completely accurate," says Bodenheimer. "It doesn't mention that there's an alternative drug that costs ten times less and is just as good."

Defenders of prescription-drug advertising suggest it's all about promoting conversations between patients and their doctors, the only people empowered to write prescriptions. But often patients simply ask for a drug, and doctors see their way clear to giving it. "Believe me there's definitely pressure," says Steinman. "Some patients will be quite insistent. Also there's just a question of time. You're always running late. It's a lot easier to say, 'Sure I'm going to give you that prescription' than to go into a lengthy explanation of why you're not going to give it." One in five consumers surveyed by AARP reported having asked their doctor about a drug the doctor didn't even know about. Few physicians would send a patient off with a script that's potentially dangerous or clearly inappropriate (one doc recalls declining to prescribe a drug for male-pattern baldness to a woman). But most often the decision falls into a "gray area," says Steinman. There might be something cheaper out there, the patient might not need *this* drug—but it's not going to hurt the patient and it'll probably help. Like the availability of free drug samples, consumer ads lower the threshold for prescribing whatever the drug companies happen to be promoting this year.

And like its approach to the doctor, the industry's engagement of consumers is becoming ever more creative, at times straining the limits of good taste. In 2000, Pfizer's adorable "Zithromax zebra," the mascot for an antibiotic used to treat the ubiquitous childhood ear infection, dangled from the stethoscopes of pediatricians and "sponsored" episodes of *Sesame Street*. This drew the fire of media watchdog group Fairness and Accuracy in Reporting, upset over the commercialization of kids' public television. It also irritated some public-health experts, since the ink was hardly dry on a recommendation by the Centers for Disease Control to use a cheaper antibiotic for ear infections. Officials of the U.S. Drug Enforcement Agency (DEA) were taken aback when in 2001, the makers of stimulants to treat kids with attention deficit hyperactivity disorder (ADHD) decided to pitch their new long-acting versions straight to moms via women's magazines and cable TV; this broke with a thirty-year-old voluntary international agreement to abstain from promoting controlled substances—drugs with addictive or abuse potential—to consumers. One DEA policy official told *USA Today* that the campaign, picturing happy kids and smiling mothers, evinced "the mentality of 'mother's little helpers' from the '60s." Likewise, breastfeeding advocates were disturbed to find the logo of a major producer of baby formula on the cover of the American Academy of Pediatrics' *New Mother's Guide to Breastfeeding.* Still others expressed doubts about the appropriateness of a new drug-ad vehicle called the Patient Channel, which would wrap the ads around educational segments about particular conditions and send them into hospital rooms, where patients lay convalescing. File this one under "Really gross, presumably rare": Warner-Lambert (now part of Pfizer) is accused in a whistle-blower lawsuit of promoting an epilepsy drug by, among other things, paying doctors to work as consultants, to participate in clinical trials—and to let drug reps watch while they examined patients, sometimes allowing the reps to make recommendations for treatment. Pfizer has denied many of the changes, which date from before it acquired Warner-Lambert.

## IN WITH THE NEW

Taken together, the drug industry's promotional tools—reps dropping samples, medical "opinion leaders" working conference halls, ads every night on TV—create an extremely powerful momentum toward the use of new brand-name drugs. With this comes the widespread assumption that the newest drug is the best drug. And sometimes it is. Other times, not.

All things being equal, some experts argue, we ought to prefer the older drug. When it comes to drugs, unlike other "hot" consumer items, there's safety to consider. We have less experience with new drugs and therefore less understanding of their risks. Premarketing clinical trials that involve a few thousand carefully selected patients can easily miss a safety problem that arises in, say, 1 in 5,000 cases. Sometimes relevant information emerges after years of general use. A 2002 study published in *JAMA* found that of all drugs with new active ingredients approved between 1975 and 1999, fully one in ten was the subject of after-the-fact warnings of serious adverse effects or was pulled from the market entirely. Half these changes took place within seven years of the drug's launch.

With these figures in mind, decisions about whether to go for the newest thing on the market should take into account whether it's truly a breakthrough with no tried-and-true alternatives and whether the condition it treats is a serious one, says the study's author, Harvard Medical School's Karen Lasser, MD. Otherwise, says Lasser, it makes sense to wait.

But public-health educators often find themselves spitting in the wind when they go up against Big Pharma's marketing juggernaut. In some cases, patients in great numbers are taking the blockbuster even while experts and best-practice guidelines recommend an older, less expensive treatment.

One might begin with the 50 million Americans who

have high blood pressure. Many will need to control this risk factor for heart disease and stroke by taking medicine every day, for years. The medical and financial stakes are high: Which medicine will they try first? On this question the Joint National Committee on Prevention, Detection, Evaluation, and Treatment of High Blood Pressure (part of the NIH) is unequivocal: The first line of treatment should be two older classes of drugs, diuretics and beta-blockers. The committee made this recommendation in 1993, and again in 1997. But the 1990s saw an increase in prescribing of another type of drug for hypertension: calcium channel-blockers (CCBs), sold under brand names like Procardia, Cardizem, and, more recently, megaseller Norvasc. Two years after the committee issued its guidelines favoring diuretics and beta-blockers, calcium channel-blockers were being prescribed about twice as often for hypertension.

As doctors debated emerging evidence on efficacy and risks of the various drugs, drugmakers wasted no time in pushing the newer and costlier brand-name CCBs. Between 1985 and 1996, ads touting CCBs in the *New England Journal of Medicine* proliferated; by 1996, they were the most heavily advertised of any medications, according to a study published in *Circulation* in 1999. Meanwhile, ads for beta-blockers declined from 12.4 percent of total ad pages in 1985 to zilch—no ads—in 1996, three years after the national committee recommended them as first-line treatment for one of the most common health conditions.

Drug-company efforts at persuasion apparently weren't confined to ad pages. When researchers at the University of Washington reported the results of a limited study showing increased rates of heart attack in patients using short-acting

CCBs versus those on diuretics and beta-blockers, the news hit the front pages, patients became alarmed, and industry people fell on the investigators like a ton of bricks. "Academic consultants to companies manufacturing calcium channel-blockers issued blistering critiques, publicly questioned the investigators' integrity, and emphasized dubious contraindications" to using the cheaper drugs, according to a report in the *New England Journal of Medicine* coauthored by the University of Washington researchers. One company issued a Freedom of Information request that demanded "all records related to study design and methodology, study protocol(s), individual data for all study results and data, data sets, statistical calculations, methodologies, and analyses" as well as meeting minutes and correspondence from researchers, staff, or oversight committees. This, from an industry that likes to keep its own minutes and data tapes to itself.

Analyzing the medical literature during a critical eighteen-month period in the controversy over CCBs, University of Toronto researchers discovered that an astounding 96 percent of commentators whose published views supported CCBs had financial ties to their manufacturers. Indeed, the industry seemed to have a hand in everywhere; over one-third of those who criticized CCBs also had ties to the companies that sold them.

Prescriptions for the specific type of CCBs that raised concerns about heart attack—short-acting versions that have to be taken more often, and in particular a drug called short-acting nifepidine—have given way to scripts for other forms of the drug, says Bodenheimer. Still, he says, "huge numbers" of people are being treated for high blood pressure with a drug that's more expensive than those recommended by official guidelines. The Norvasc web site, featuring a lean middle-aged man on a diving board, calls the drug "the most prescribed cardiovascular agent in the world."

Drug companies tend not to sponsor research that pits their products directly against other drugs, especially cheaper ones. Therefore, it took the federal government mounting the most ambitious hypertension trial ever to finally bring attention to the merits of older blood-pressure drugs. Published in *JAMA* in December 2002, the study found that a diuretic—the "water pill" that's been around for half a century and costs pennies a pill—was slightly more effective than CCBs and ACE inhibitors (another relatively new and pricey drug) at preventing heart attacks and other complications of hypertension. "[T]here is no cost-quality tradeoff; the most effective therapy was also the least expensive," said a *JAMA* editorial accompanying the study. "Many of the newer drugs were approved because they reduce blood pressure and the risk of heart disease compared with a placebo. But they were not tested against each other," said National Heart, Lung and Blood Institute director Claude Lenfant, MD, in announcing the study's results. "Yet, these more costly medications were often promoted as having advantages over older drugs, which contributed to the rapid escalation of their use." Had diuretic use not dropped off precipitously following the introduction of pricier alternatives, researchers estimated, hypertension scripts during the ensuing decade would have cost $3.1 billion less. The government's study suggests the cheaper scripts would also have resulted in better health for Americans with high blood pressure.

A more recent example of fleet drug-industry promotions matched against the slow-grinding wheels of research and expert debate involves the extraordinarily rapid adoption by the American public of drugs called selective COX-2 inhibitors—Vioxx and Celebrex—to treat arthritis pain. Both have been among the drugs most intensively advertised to consumers and among the biggest contributors to increased spending for prescription drugs, with sales of each topping $2 billion in 2001. Typically, a prescription costs between $80 and $100. Far more expensive but apparently no better at reducing pain than generic ibuprofen or naproxen, the new drugs' main selling point is their lower risk profile; they're less likely to cause stomach problems like ulcers.

But as noted earlier, the main study proving this benefit from Celebrex abandoned six months' worth of data in reaching its conclusions. An editorial published in June 2002 in the influential *British Medical Journal* took the authors of the Celebrex study to task for "serious irregularities" in the research, including "post hoc changes in design, outcomes, and analysis." The editorial also noted that in spite of its flaws, the study had achieved widespread currency in the medical world: Thirty thousand copies had been ordered from the publisher, and the study had been cited 169 times in the professional literature.

As for Vioxx, the single most advertised drug in 2000, an important trial did find that it caused fewer serious gastrointestinal problems than the comparison drug, naproxen—but the study also turned up an unexplained four- to fivefold increase in heart attacks in the Vioxx group. In 2001, the FDA sent Merck & Co. a warning letter: "You have engaged in a promotional campaign for Vioxx that minimizes the potentially serious cardiovascular findings that were observed in the Vioxx Gastrointestinal Outcomes Research (VIGOR) study," the letter said. Among the promotional materials referred to in the letter is a May 2001 press release entitled "Merck Confirms Favorable Cardiovascular Safety Profile of Vioxx." The FDA called the claim "simply incomprehensible." It may be that the comparison drug naproxen actually protects the heart and thus made Vioxx look bad. Nevertheless, although new FDA-approved labeling for Vioxx moderates warnings on stomach problems, it adds information about possible heart effects.

Use of newer, powerful antibiotics to treat simple infections may also be influenced by advertising. "Antibiotics are promoted pretty heavily to doctors through magazine ads and exhibits at conferences," says Elbert Huang, MD, of the University of Chicago. "It's very evident nobody promotes generics." This troubles public-health specialists not only because the new drugs tend to cost more but also because using the big guns when they're not required could promote the development of antibiotic-resistant organisms. For these reasons, the Infectious Disease Society of America recommends treating ordinary urinary tract infections (UTIs) with an older antibiotic, trimethoprim-sulphamethoxazole (trade names Bactrim, Septra, also available as a generic). But according to a recent study by Huang published in the *Archives of Internal Medicine,* use of the recommended antibiotic for urinary tract infections has declined over the last decade from 48 percent in 1989–1990 to only 24 percent in 1997–1998. Meanwhile, UTI scripts for another class of antibiotics, fluoroquinolones such as Cipro, rose from 19 percent to 29 percent. Bayer recently applied to the FDA for approval of a special dosage form of Cipro—Cipro UTI—which, the company says, "can be used to effectively treat uncomplicated urinary tract infections in only three days." Except in areas where there are high rates of pathogen resistance to it, the older and far less expensive drug is likely to do just as well. "In the garden-variety UTI, Bactrim works in the same three-day period that Cipro works," says Huang.

### IN WITH THE NEW—FASTER!

When weighing whether to approve a new drug for marketing, the FDA must strive for efficiency—so that patients don't wait too long for breakthrough medicines—but also, of course, for safety.

The Prescription Drug User Fee Act (PDUFA), first implemented in 1992, was meant to speed up a regulatory-review procedure that had delayed the introduction of important drugs for AIDS and other scourges. In the process, it created a new relationship between the drug industry and the agency that regulates it: Under PDUFA, the FDA collects fees from drug companies to pay the salaries of the very people who approve or reject their products for marketing. In exchange for the fees, the FDA is required to meet strict deadlines for review of all drugs, even those not anxiously awaited by patients.

The measure has succeeded in accelerating review and is hailed by the drug industry and FDA alike as a success. "The fees have enabled the FDA to pay the salaries of more than 1,000 highly-qualified reviewers and to cut the review time for new drugs almost in half since 1991, from 30.3 months at that time to 16.4 months in 2001," PhRMA said in a June 2002 press release. Because patents are typically obtained well before FDA review even begins, a quicker review lengthens a drug's effective patent life, that is, the time it can be *sold* under patent.

The FDA has handled more applications since PDUFA took force and has approved a higher percentage of those applications, about 80 percent at the end of the 1990s, versus less than 60 percent in the years before PDUFA. Whereas in the early 1990s a new drug was rarely introduced first in the United States, now more than half launch here.

None of these facts means more dangerous drugs are clearing FDA review. The rate of drug withdrawals has remained steady at 2.7 percent, the agency says. This is rather disconcerting, though: Of fifty-three FDA reviewers who responded to a Public Citizen survey in late 1998 (172 were contacted), nineteen identified a total of twenty-seven newly approved drugs they had worked on that, in their opinion, should not have been approved.

With PDUFA set to expire in the fall, PhRMA and the FDA privately hammered out an agreement for an expanded version in the spring of 2002, which Congress passed in June, overwhelmingly and with little debate. The reauthorization spared the FDA from having to lay off reviewers that summer. It also increased drug-company fees, adding 500 new reviewers to the FDA payroll. The new PDUFA for the first time allows FDA to use drug-company fees to help monitor the safety of drugs *after* market launch as well as before.

Whatever one makes of this balance between speed and caution in the introduction and uptake of new drugs, it seems a particularly American trait to greet the "new and improved" fruits of science and industry with enthusiastic approval. We like the idea of smarter and more powerful medicines, much the same way we like the idea of more horses under the hood or a handier way to mop the kitchen floor. And we're often right to appreciate innovation; after all, the water pills that continue to impress researchers with their anti-hypertensive properties were once the newest wonder drug. We also have a lot of faith in ourselves as individuals, believing that each of us can, in consultation with a physician, simply try a drug and decide its merits for ourselves. And surely this sense of independence serves us well in many instances. But like the physicians who believed their colleagues were influenced by pharmaceutical-industry pitches while they themselves were immune, American consumers sometimes underestimate the extent to which we are all susceptible to the vagaries of human psychology, to the assumptions of our culture, and to the insistent tide of economic incentives that are built into our health-care system.

# chapter 6

# DRUGS R US

YOU'D ALMOST have to have spent the last few years under a rock not to recognize the name Claritin. It's the first "non-sedating antihistamine," the one, if you believe the seemingly ubiquitous ads, that allows allergy sufferers to gambol through fields of flowers with nary a symptom. As one of the first intensive consumer advertising campaigns for a prescription drug—Schering-Plough spent $421 million on it from 1998 to 2000—its yield could not have been more encouraging to other companies poised to enter the fray. Sales of Claritin products nearly doubled during those years, with Claritin tablets and fast-acting RediTabs bringing in well over $2 billion in 2001. In a 2000 survey by IMS Health, which tracks the pharmaceutical industry, half of allergy sufferers reported that an ad had led them to talk with a doctor. A survey of doctors found that across all drug classes, Claritin was the most often requested product.

In the spring of 1999, journalist Stephen S. Hall, like so many others, tried Claritin. Two years and numerous interviews and Freedom of Information requests later, Hall reported in the *New York Times Magazine*, "The little white pill was easy to swallow and had to be taken only once a day. There was just one problem: it didn't work." Hall had discovered that in studies submitted to the FDA for approval of the drug, Claritin patients reported relatively modest improvements in symptoms. At the same time, as is often the case in studies of allergy medicines, those on placebo had done quite well. In one trial, for example, Claritin users had reported a 46-percent improvement in symptoms, while placebo had produced a 35-percent improvement. One FDA reviewer had suggested a higher dose was called for, but Claritin in higher doses might produce the same muddle-headed feeling that troubled users of much cheaper over-the-counter antihistamines, depriving Schering-Plough of a critical selling point. As Hall's less-than-flattering portrait of the blockbuster gained currency, Schering-Plough responded by insisting its ads adhered to FDA regulations and that moreover, in the words of a company spokesperson, "no amount of marketing . . . can sustain a drug that's not effective."

Drugmakers have always had to spend a relatively large sum on marketing for every dollar of sales, in part, marketing experts explain, because medicines are "experience" goods. Unlike, say, microwaves or paper clips, you have to try the pill before you know what it has to offer. The Schering-Plough spokesperson's comment calls on the widely held assumption that the "experience" of a drug is cut-and-dried, based entirely on the product's inherent properties: Drugs either "work" or "don't work." Mostly, we assume they work. But medicines are a lot more complicated than paper clips or, for that matter, many other experience goods, for instance, snack foods or cosmetics. There's a range in how reliably a given pharmaceutical produces the desired effect. Anti-hypertensive drugs and cholesterol-lowering drugs reduce blood pressure and cholesterol in just about everybody, if to varying degrees. Other drugs seem to work in one out of two people. An analysis of 117 trials of ulcer medicines reported healing rates ranging from 38 percent to 100 percent. Often, differences in response are based on personal factors that aren't predictable or well understood. But we do know that, for example, the same drug is likely to work differently in an elderly person than in a child or young adult. Men may respond differently than women.

And this may be the most complicating factor of all: What we hope and believe about a medicine matters—in the decision about whether to try a drug in the first place, but perhaps also in how we experience its effects. What we've come to know through past experience shapes whether we attribute healing to this drug, that drug, or some entirely separate factor. Indeed, culture and personal philosophy influence what we interpret as disease and whether we believe the disease is appropriately treated—or treatable at all—with medicine. Finally, medicines are unique among commercial products in that, in certain circumstances, people believe access to them is a human right. Especially in market-oriented America, these products exist at a highly charged crossroads for individuals and for society: How much health for how much money? Whose health? Whose money?

Can marketing sell a drug that's not very effective? It's certainly possible. The taking of medicine is an ancient practice that was once inseparable from myth and ritual—think of Chiron, Greek teacher of pharmacy, half human and half horse—and it contains an element of these to this day. Everything from a pill's trade name (*Claritin* for example invokes the word *clarify*, to make comprehensible, clear, and pure) to its shape and color (small, white) to the images (woman grinning among pollen-heavy flowers) that come to be associated with a drug help give it meaning that may support or extend its pharmacological effects. Not every marketing effort works. Successful strategies recognize and harness the deepest impulses of those they address. As one drug marketing specialist writing in the journal *DTC Perspectives* exhorts colleagues, "Ultimately, have you created an experience so empathetic and motivating that sufferers will vault over fair balance and gird themselves for doctors' visits so they can get to the person they want to be? Aided and abetted by your brand, positively reinforced by your messages and supported for the long haul by your tireless attention and contact, are your customers ready for the relationship that will change their lives?"

Placebo-controlled trials—the scientific method accepted as the best way to test effectiveness—isolate a drug's pharmacological effects. Conversely, the study of the placebo effect itself can be seen as an inquiry into psychological and cultural factors that influence our expectations of and response to medicine. Anthropologist Daniel E. Moerman, Ph.D., of the University of Michigan, calls it "the meaning response." In a recent review, Moerman describes an array of research findings that suggest the breadth of this response: Two inert pills produce a more robust placebo response than one. Inert capsules have been shown to be more effective than inert tablets, whereas injected placebos have worked better than pills in studies of hypertension, rheumatoid arthritis, and migraine headaches. Blue and green placebos are more likely to have a sedative effect, red and orange tablets to stimulate. Moerman points out that in one Italian study of placebos as sedatives, women responded to blue tablets, but the same tablets actually kept men awake—perhaps, he muses, because of the color's association with their national soccer team. (He notes as well that Viagra, a blue lozenge usually depicted pointing upward and to the right, may trade on the color's connotation of indecency, as in "blue movie.") In controlled trials, so-called active placebos that mimic the study drug's side effects often stimulate a more robust response than totally inert pills. Side effects mean the drug is working.

Research strongly suggests that messages you get from the person who offers a drug can affect how you respond to it. In one study, whether the practitioner "undersold" or "oversold" an inert "painkiller" was by far the biggest factor affecting placebo response. Good doctors use this in their work all the time, aware that medicines go farther with a dose of optimism. As Gerstein puts it, "It's a very legitimate medical tool to say, 'This is a very excellent drug, it's really going to help you.'" Similarly, doctors since the nineteenth century have traded the wry advice to hurry up and use new drugs while they still work, acknowledging that the effectiveness of older drugs tends to decline as new ones are introduced to replace them. If response to drugs (or placebos) can vary over time, it also sometimes varies by geography or, perhaps, culture. In Moerman's analysis of ulcer trials, placebo healing averaged 59 percent among Germans but only 22 percent among their neighbors in Denmark and the Netherlands.

For our purposes, one of the most interesting studies in Moerman's review involves the impact of "branding." British women who used painkillers for headache were assigned to one of four treatment groups: aspirin labeled with a widely advertised brand, the same aspirin in plain packaging, placebo labeled with the widely advertised brand, or unbranded placebo. They were asked to rate their pain relief from –1 for "worse" to +4 for "completely better." The real drug—even when unbranded—provided more relief than any placebo. But branding boosted pain relief for both the active drug and the inert tablet. Among women taking brand-name placebo, 64 percent reported relief from their headaches, versus 55 percent of those taking plain-package placebo. "Aspirin relieves headaches," writes Moerman. "But so does the knowledge that the pills you are taking are good ones, which you learned on TV."

For years, researchers labored to identify the personality of a typical "placebo responder." Weak-minded perhaps? But they labored in vain. Although not all conditions are susceptible to placebo treatments, it seems that given the right circumstances, most people are. As one author on the subject put it, "We have met the placebo responder and he is us."

The case of antidepressant medication is perhaps the supreme example in which commercial forces, medical science, contemporary culture, and the vivid crucible of personal experience combine to create a controversial drug phenomenon. Antidepressants, both the older-generation tricyclics and the newer selective serotonin reuptake inhibitors (SSRIs), have similar efficacy—they tend to work in at least half the people who try them. And depression itself is relatively responsive to placebo. Thus, as in the Claritin studies, studies of antidepressants sometimes demonstrate a rather slender spread between placebo and drug response.

What does this mean? Some experts think that the large placebo response simply masks separate and substantial pharmacological effects of antidepressant medicine or that certain studies fail to tease out great benefits over placebo in select patients or do not identify particularly potent medications. Others think the difference between placebo and active drug, though modest, is significant. And some suspect that, indeed, the ability of antidepressants to call off the black dog rests largely on the power of placebo. "The problem is not that you don't get a response," says University of Connecticut psychologist Irving Kirsch, Ph.D. "The problem is that you don't know whether the effect is due to the drug or due to the person's belief in the drug. It's such a nice large response that you get, to medication or placebo. When somebody tries one of these and they get better, they naturally ascribe it to whatever they've tried. Doctors see their patients respond very well and so they too become convinced."

Kirsch is the author of a controversial analysis of antidepressant effectiveness published in July 2002 in *Prevention and Treatment,* a journal of the American Psychological Association. He used a Freedom of Information request to obtain studies submitted to the FDA for approval of the six most widely prescribed antidepressants approved between 1987 and 1999—Prozac, Paxil, Zoloft, Effexor, Serzone, and

Celexa. On average, about 80 percent of the response to medication was duplicated in the placebo groups, Kirsch reports. On a commonly used fifty-point scale measuring symptoms of depression, people getting active medicine improved an average of two points more than placebo patients. Meanwhile, other research has shown that typical response to given antidepressants—and to dummy pills in antidepressant studies—has increased significantly in recent years. Kirsch remarks, "It's probably because of greater publicity about the effectiveness of antidepressants."

There can be no doubt that drug companies helped propel this publicity, funding depression screenings and advocacy groups, and encouraging people to seek treatment through a blizzard of advertising and other literature. Eli Lilly spent $41 million advertising Prozac to consumers in 1998, nearly double what it spent the year before. Competitor Glaxo-SmithKline upped the ante, spending $91.8 million advertising Paxil to consumers in 2000. In the fall of 2002, Wyeth, the maker of Effexor, launched forums on college campuses entitled "Depression in College: Real World, Real Life, Real Issues." A young reality-TV star (who takes Effexor) was a featured speaker.

Popular media have also done their bit. Two years after the launch of Prozac in 1988, the pill was on the cover of *Newsweek* and *Time*. The 1993 book *Listening to Prozac* told stories of people transformed by the drug and gave currency to the term "cosmetic psychopharmacology," a sort of personality lift via medication. According to a recent review of media treatment of antidepressants by Michael Montagne, R.Ph., Ph.D., a professor of pharmacy at Massachusetts College of Pharmacy and Allied Health Services, terms commonly used to describe Prozac included "the Happy Pill," "the Feel-Good Pill," and "the Personality Pill." What's not to like? Moerman observes that even incidents like one near his hometown in which a crazed teacher shot the school principal and claimed Prozac made him do it (a defense that failed) add to the drug's mystique: "You come away thinking, *Wow, that Prozac, that's powerful stuff.*"

Antidepressant sales spiked from $2 billion in 1993 to more than $12 billion by 2001, prescribed increasingly by non-psychiatrists and for a wider array of conditions, including so-called minor depression (in which efficacy is less well-established than in major depression) and, according to a review recently published in *Health Affairs*, anxiety, obsessive-compulsive disorder, bulimia, panic disorders, post-traumatic stress disorder, premenstrual syndrome, weight loss, and smoking cessation. Before Prozac dropped out, three antidepressants were among the top ten best-selling drugs in America. According to an ABC News poll, one in eight Americans took an antidepressant at some point during the 1990s.

Is all of this new and various antidepressant use, as medical professionals put it, "appropriate"? Is it working? Who's to say? Kirsch believes that given the risk of side effects with medication, it should not be the "first-strike option" for depression. In his paper, he evokes the metaphor of "the emperor's new clothes," suggesting a reluctance by many to admit how paltry the evidence is for SSRIs' effectiveness. Moerman prefers "the loaves and the fishes," which gives a sense of bounteous good that flows, however implausibly, from slim rations. This might be seen as a reinterpretation of the term "miracle drug," for while Moerman does not believe in the pharmacological power of SSRIs, he has seen that when his wife, Claudine Ferrand, takes Zoloft, she is free of the severe depression to which she had been prey. And here we return to drugs as a uniquely complex "experience" product.

Ferrand, for her part, is well aware of the research on antidepressants and placebo. She admits to an occasional uneasiness, a feeling that perhaps she's been cheated somehow. She can chuckle at the suggestion that her desire to get out of a dismal depression clinic twenty years ago might have stimulated her first dramatic response to the early generation antidepressant imipramine. But she soon grows serious. "It was much more than that. I mean, I'm telling you. I could laugh again, I could open my mouth without crying. There were a lot of things that had been gone from my life. Personally, I believe it's the medication that did it."

Depression, described in various ways through history and across cultures, seems an all but universal component of human experience. But this is not necessarily true of all diseases or disorders. In her 1988 book *Medicine and Culture*, medical writer Lynn Payer describes a German preoccupation with the heart and circulation, accompanied by a very high rate of diagnosis of *Herzinsuffizienz*, a form of "cardiac insufficiency" that "would not be considered a disease in England, France, or America." Doctors in Germany are at pains to treat the problem in its earliest stages with digitalis or other cardiac drugs; some consider any man over sixty to have "latent heart insufficiency." Among the French, Payer documents a once intense though waning focus on liver crisis, *crise de foie*. An array of ailments from migraines to asthma to gastrointestinal upsets have been attributed to the French liver or various abnormalities of the bile duct; according to Payer, in 1970 the French pharmacopoeia included 300 liver drugs, accounting for 5 percent of drug consumption. And to Americans Payer attributes a preoccupation with the body as a sublime machine subject to invasion by germs, matched by an enthusiasm for blasting the invaders with antibiotics.

But Payer's central conclusion about American medicine is that it is uncommonly aggressive. Compared with Europeans, Americans perform more tests to identify disease. Although often favoring surgery over drug therapy (a preference that has changed considerably since Payer's book came out in the 1980s), when Americans do use drugs they tend to use more aggressive medicines in higher doses. They prefer to use whatever works faster and, above all, to insist upon treatment itself, even for the most hopeless cases. One English doctor told Payer, "I call them the Godsakers. 'For God's sake *do* something.'"

## IF YOU BUILD IT . . .

If the ways people define and understand disease differ by culture, they can also, of course, change over time. Pharmaceutical companies have a profound influence on this process—by inventing drugs where none existed before; by designing clinical research to position those drugs in the marketplace; by funding patient and professional groups that, in turn, speak through the popular media; and by tirelessly promoting awareness of their medicines and the ailments they're designed to treat. In some cases, drug companies vastly increase the market in a disease class; in other cases, they create new markets. "The 'build it and they will come' mentality has served many companies well," as one writer in *Pharmaceutical Executive* puts it. An executive in drugs marketing, participating in a roundtable talk published in the same journal, says it more boldly: "[H]ow many people knew ten years ago that there would be such a term as 'erectile dysfunction'? That's brilliant branding. And it's not just about branding the drug; it's branding the condition and, by inference, a branding of the patient . . . What kind of patient does a blockbuster create? We're creating patient populations just as we're creating medicines, to make sure that products become blockbusters."

In other words, erectile dysfunction is now, like Viagra, Pfizer's baby. And a curious thing is happening. The Viagra patient, once exemplified by Bob Dole, the very image of dignified but wounded virility after his election loss to Bill Clinton, has morphed into Rafael Palmeiro of the Texas Rangers, looking buff in his tight-fitting uniform, with a tag line that compares sex to baseball: "I take infield practice: 3 Gold Gloves. I take Viagra. Let's just say it works for me." Let anyone accuse Pfizer of promoting the recreational use of Viagra and someone else will invoke the first image, citing the undertreatment and long neglect of this embarrassing problem. But can't they both be right?

When industry creates new markets for its products, is it simply raising awareness of an existing condition for which treatment has not been available? Emphasizing a particular diagnosis or label for certain symptoms? Is this "disease-mongering," as Australian writer Ray Moynihan has argued in the *British Medical Journal*, in order to sell drugs to essentially healthy people? Perhaps all of the above, depending on the situation. One thing we do know. Drug-company campaigns to raise awareness among doctors and consumers about a given disease or dysfunction carry an implicit proposal for cure. No sooner do you learn of the condition than you see a drug-company logo or hear the name of its drug.

Moynihan's daring piece describes what he calls a "global 'makeover'" of irritable bowel syndrome (IBS) by a medical communications firm working to market GlaxoSmith Kline's Lotronex (which was withdrawn from the market because of safety problems not long after its 2000 launch but was allowed to go back on sale in 2002 under strict FDA-mandated use restrictions). Acknowledging that the condition is severely disabling in some people, Moynihan argues that the company's educational program aimed to recruit the many for whom IBS is a troublesome but relatively benign set of symptoms. He quotes from a draft marketing strategy, leaked from the PR firm, that outlines plans to set up a professional advisory board, develop "best practice guidelines" for diagnosing and managing IBS, and publish a newsletter on it: "IBS must be established in the minds of doctors as a significant and discrete disease state ... [Patients also] need to be convinced that IBS is a common and recognized medical disorder."

More lately, Moynihan has written about the industry's sponsorship of conferences on "female sexual dysfunction" (FSD) that he says are aimed at salting the ground for future companion drugs to Viagra. One supplement maker is already capitalizing on the buzz; its magazine ad, designed to mimic a prescription-drug ad with its accompanying small print, claims that "an astounding 43 percent of women" have suffered from FSD, which in its mildest form is characterized by "a slight decrease in interest." Compulsive shopping, meanwhile, is the newest research focus for one antidepressant maker.

Hormone replacement therapy (HRT) is one of the more dazzling examples of this "build it and they will come" phenomenon—not only because the drugs turned out to be potentially harmful but also because vast numbers of women have taken them to prevent health problems associated with a "risk factor" that literally every woman on earth will experience if she lives long enough: menopause. By the time estrogen use took off in the 1960s, it had been sporadically prescribed, and its role in women's health had been studied, for decades. It wasn't research that launched HRT. It was an idea, a theory that turned our way of understanding health and medicine on its head, casting menopause, on the one hand, as an unnatural deficiency and hormone pills, on the other hand, as a natural restorative, more supplement than drug.

Gynecologist Robert Wilson's 1966 book *Feminine Forever* followed a by now familiar bad news–good news story line: An extraordinarily widespread health threat has gone unrecognized but, happily, has a ready solution. In this case the message seems to have begun not as a drug-company marketing scheme but as a personal crusade, with Wilson recruiting the makers of sex hormones to support not only his book but also his foundation and many public appearances. "He called me in my office," recalls Tom Vecchio, MD, a onetime manager at Upjohn. "He wanted to promote this theory to the public. I was hesitant because the evidence was pretty scanty and he just threw a tantrum on the phone and called me all kind of names and insisted on speaking to the boss."

Wilson's work seems, by today's standards, transparently misogynist, even disturbed. He called menopause a state of "living decay," unabashedly touting estrogen as a way to make older women more attractive and "pleasant to live with." "It is the case of the untreated woman—the prematurely aging castrate—that is unnatural," he wrote. Says Cynthia Pearson, head of the National Women's Health Network and a coauthor of the prescient book *The Truth About Hormone Replacement Therapy,* "I guess we would need to put ourselves in a little time warp to be able to reabsorb the culture of the time. This was *Dick Van Dyke* and *Bonanza.* This was a time when adult women were called girls and women couldn't get credit in their own names and couldn't serve on juries in some states."

Drugmakers ran with Wilson's message, confirming the life stage of menopause as an encompassing disaster. National Public Radio recently quoted from a 1972 promotional film: "The physical alterations that are associated with the menopause may induce emotional changes. When a woman develops hot flashes, sweats, wrinkles on her face, she is quite concerned that she is losing her youth—that she may indeed be losing her husband." Another ad from the 1970s, quoted in an article by journalist and women's health activist Barbara Seaman, showed a father and children looking aghast at something the family's distraught middle-aged mother has just done: "Almost any tranquilizer might calm her down," read the copy, "but at her age, estrogen may be what she really needs." Estrogen soon became one of the most-prescribed drugs in America.

It fell briefly from grace and out of widespread use after research in the mid-1970s suggested an association with uterine cancer—only to be revived during the 1980s when studies indicated that coupling estrogen with another hormone, progestin, canceled this risk. HRT got a further boost in the 1980s when several products won FDA approval for prevention of one long-term health risk: osteoporosis.

Hormones once again were heralded as a panacea, but the message was reformed for a new generation, this time appealing to health-conscious concerns about disease prevention and women's determination to remain vital beyond middle age. The new company pitchwomen for HRT, Patti Labelle and Lauren Hutton, were the objects of admiration, not contempt. HRT would not only help women get past the hot flashes and other symptoms of menopause (including, Hutton broadly hinted to *Parade Magazine,* looking older and feeling cranky) but, used long-term, it would also protect them from Alzheimer's, heart disease, stroke, osteoporosis, and colon cancer. The question became, why *wouldn't* you take it? Indeed, one ad in a medical publication urged doctors, "If your menopausal patients have new questions about menopause . . . consider the entire body of evidence," with arrows pointing to, according to Pearson, the uterus, the breast, the brain, the skin, the bone, and the teeth.

Drugmakers got across unproved claims through what Pearson calls "soft marketing," but in general they were much more constrained than doctors, since FDA regulates what they can and can't say about their products. Wyeth-Ayerst applied in 1990 for FDA permission to sell estrogen as a heart-disease preventative, but the FDA found the claim came up short on evidence and turned it down. One sixty-year-old urbanite recalls her gynecologist sending her home with a drug-company video about HRT; she noticed that the film was careful to claim only that HRT prevented bone loss and hot flashes. But the doc was leaning on her to take hormones for what had become their most important supposed benefit: heart disease prevention. This was the early 1990s. "I'd read enough to be suspicious of the whole universe of hormone replacement therapy," says Gloria. "But my gynecologist and everybody else made me feel like I was essentially suicidal if I didn't take it. It's really a lot of pressure."

A 2000 market-research report on drugs for women reflects with some disapproval that although there were a whopping 40 million women over age fifty, only 20 to 30 percent of those "eligible" for HRT were taking it. "The primary reason that women are not taking HRT," says the report, "is that many do not see the need due to lack of education on the risk of cardiovascular disease and osteoporosis."

Others might see these figures in an altogether different light: After all, spending on HRT had surged by 219 percent between 1995 and 1998 alone, according to one study. For a number of years, Wyeth-Ayerst's Premarin posted the best sales figures of any drug product sold in America. Notwithstanding protests from animal-rights groups, Wyeth even managed to turn to its advantage the fact that its Premarin-family products are derived from the urine of pregnant mares, convincing the FDA, with the help of women's groups, not to approve a plant-based generic on the grounds that it was missing a key ingredient whose significance no one seemed able to identify. According to a recent report in

*Business Week,* the Premarin family came to account for 15 percent of Wyeth's sales, and as much as 30 percent of its profits. In the spring of 2002, Wyeth launched a sixtieth anniversary celebration of Premarin, commissioning photographs of accomplished middle-aged women who used hormone products, to be circulated to museums, galleries, and medical meetings across the country. "More than 11 million women take a Premarin Family Product on a daily basis, and this exhibit tries to take that statistic and make it a little bit more personal," according to the company press release.

A few months later, the federal government stopped its trial of estrogen-progestin (Prempro) in healthy menopausal women, years ahead of schedule. Yes, the treatment helped to prevent some baddies: The study confirmed HRT's protection against bone fractures and added conclusive evidence of protection from colon cancer. But the massive Women's Health Initiative (WHI) also showed that HRT creates increased risk for invasive breast cancer, blood clots, and indeed, coronary heart disease and stroke, risks that, while statistically slight, clearly trump any preventive benefits. Sales of Prempro dropped more than 50 percent in the months following the news, and sales of Premarin suffered, too, if less dramatically. Gloria has been off hormones for years; now most of her friends are, too, though they still debate the subject, sometimes heatedly. One friend is sticking with HRT in the hope that it will prevent Alzheimer's, one of the few major claims for hormones that remains to be proven or disproven. Gloria remembers, "I kept saying to her, 'Okay, they *stopped* the trial. That's a sure thing.' But I think she may fear losing her mind more than she fears anything else."

Drug-company-sponsored thinking about menopause as a deficiency—an idea that set medical research and practice along the path of studying and giving hormones almost as if to prevent aging itself—was specious from the beginning. That the evidence for HRT turned negative in the end only reinforces the premise that one ought to be staunchly conservative about advising healthy people to take systemic medications on a daily basis for years on end to prevent diseases they might never get. The idea that menopause triggers the need for pharmacological disease prevention not only got lots of women taking pills, but it led to a huge devotion of resources to finding out whether those pills in fact prevented disease. "It's really frustrating that the company making the most-often prescribed product grosses over a billion dollars a year on that product—$2.1 billion on the whole family—and the federal government has to pay the tab on finding out whether its current pattern of use is more harmful than helpful," Pearson laments. "It's just such a wrong ordering of priorities and accountability."

The irony is that the WHI results, though relevant to anyone considering hormone therapy, bear least on the situation of women interested in HRT for its core indication—to provide relatively short-term relief from intolerable menopausal symptoms. The risks for an individual are small and seem to accumulate over time. In fact, a few months after the study was stopped, the NIH announced that the term "hormone replacement therapy" should be abandoned in favor of the more accurate "menopausal hormone therapy." The drugs never "replaced" anything; they restored neither the disease-risk profile of youth, nor its reproductive capacity. "It was almost as though the language was corrupting thought," Barnett Kramer, MD, director of the NIH Office of Disease Prevention, told *The New York Times*.

By the way, when's the last time you heard the term "dowager's hump"? Try Merck's web site for its nonhormonal osteoporosis drug Fosamax. In the year following the drug's launch, doctor visits for osteoporosis doubled. "Early on, osteoporosis is a silent disease, *so you may not see any signs*," the web site observes. A list of risk factors begins, "Are you past menopause?" and ends with these words of advice: "Remember: Menopause is a key factor contributing to the development of osteoporosis. Even if none of these risk factors applies to you, you may still have or develop osteoporosis if you're a woman past menopause. Ask your health-care provider whether a bone density test may be right for you." Not surprisingly, Merck's Bone Measurement Institute, a nonprofit subsidiary, has advocated for Medicare to cover bone-density testing and has worked to educate doctors about the technology. "Help change the future of your post menopausal patients with osteoporosis," the institute's web site tells them. "Many are currently receiving treatment—all other post menopausal women are at risk."

How different is this from saying all men over sixty have latent cardiac insufficiency? The benefits of biophosphonates like Fosamax are highest for those at highest risk for bone fracture—older women with especially fragile bones or previous fractures. And though the drugs increase bone mass quickly, it's not clear that building bone mass early on prevents fractures a decade or two down the road. The U.S. Preventive Services Task Force recently recommended all women be screened for osteoporosis beginning at sixty-five. According to the task force's calculations, among women sixty-five to sixty-nine, eighty-eight individuals with low bone density would need to take medication for five years to prevent one hip fracture, a number that would decline as the women got older. But Fosamax ads show athletic women who don't look a day older than fifty, at which point, typically, that risk factor menopause rears its head. "With every medication there's a benefit-harm trade-off," says Heidi D. Nelson, MD, who along with colleagues at Oregon Health and Science University analyzed the evidence for the task force. "Whenever the benefit is potentially large and the harms small, the ratio leans towards treatment. But if the benefits are small and the harms exist, the ratio may be unfavorable. It's hard to justify the use of biophosphonates for most healthy 50-year-old women. The emphasis on these drugs is displaced among younger 'worried well' women," says Nelson, employing a public-health term that describes those who are highly motivated to seek treatment but may not need it.

## POPPING PILLS AND TAKING OUR MEDICINE

It has been suggested that the impulse to use drugs is universal, a trait that distinguishes human beings from other animals. And isn't there something inherently appealing about taking medicine? You swallow it—you get better. Getting a medicine defines and validates one's suffering, while offering the promise of a solution. Indeed, though the term "drug hunger" most often describes the cravings of addiction, Jerry Avorn, MD, of Harvard Medical School, has applied it to the cold sufferer who won't be satisfied without a prescription for an antibiotic (even though the cold's likely cause is a virus that won't respond to antibiotics). "In a real sense," writes Avorn in *Annals of Internal Medicine,* "the drug prescription prolongs the physician-patient encounter by enabling the patient to ingest 'a dose of the doctor' several times a day." Ironically, doctors under pressure from insurers to manage costs have an incentive to get busy and write a script—an "office-visit-terminating event," as physician Ralph Gonzales quips.

And the feeling they're getting the bum's rush may leave patients with an even greater desire for that take-away dose of attention. Gonzales, an expert in appropriate antibiotic use at the University of California, San Francisco, and author of *Practice Guidelines in Primary Care,* cites a study in which patients who felt they were treated with respect and care by a physician were satisfied without a prescription. But some of those who came away with a prescription were satisfied even if they didn't feel well-treated by the doc. Patients, like doctors, are busy and may perceive drugs, especially acute-care medicines like antibiotics, as the no-nonsense means to an end. "The public view antibiotics as very powerful medicine, the strongest medicine we have for infections," says Gonzales. "If there's even a remote chance that the antibiotic might help them, they want it. And they want it because they need to get back to work, or back to their usual activity level."

There's also an important—and, for many people, advantageous—movement under way toward the use of medications to manage chronic conditions. As noted earlier, there are many more medicines available for these conditions. Partly as a result of research demonstrating the benefits of the new meds, guidelines for treating conditions like hypertension, high cholesterol, diabetes, and osteoporosis have been broadened. Add to these factors the aging population. As baby boomers pass middle age, the percentage of North Americans sixty-five and older is expected to climb from 12.5 percent in 2000 to 20.3 percent in 2030. These new old people promise to be a different, more "proactive" breed. "My grandmother didn't like to take drugs. They came about during her lifetime," says J. Lyle Bootman, Ph.D., dean of the College of Pharmacy at the University of Arizona. "Now it's a totally different attitude: you've got an ailment, take a pill, you want to feel good, take a pill, you want more hair, take a pill. . . . The bottom line is, we're going to have increased consumption."

Or as Beth Greck, Pharm.D., a pharmacist in Ashland, North Carolina, puts it: "We're making more drugs for more things. Every time the heart failure guidelines come out, there's a new medication. So if somebody has heart failure and diabetes, all of a sudden there are your ten medications. We have evidence that these medicines work, so we have to give them. Then what happens is you start treating side effects with another medication."

Not only are more people taking drugs, but it's becoming more common for individuals to take six, eight, or more prescriptions and over-the-counter medicines on a regular basis. Even when they're all effective, safe, and indicated in themselves, together they may simply be too much—physically, practically, and perhaps financially. "Typically, if you're unmanaged and taking eight or more prescription drugs, there's virtually 100-percent probability of having a drug-drug interaction that will have a negative impact on your health," says Wayne K. Anderson, Ph.D., dean of the School of Pharmacy and Pharmaceutical Sciences at the University of Buffalo.

When David Morris, MD, retired from a long career in academic medicine a few years ago to work in a nursing home in Riverdale, New York, he was "amazed" to see how drugs were being distributed. "If you have gas or sneeze or have an itch, a medicine is dispensed," he says. Morris began reviewing residents' medications—it was typical for them to be on eleven different drugs—and (if the patient was amenable) winnowing them down. He was able to monitor patients on a daily basis, so if, for example, someone's blood pressure went up after stopping the meds, he could start the patient on them again. But Morris says in the great majority of cases, nothing happened. In fact, some patients were relieved of disturbances in balance, sleep, or appetite.

Unrecognized drug side effects are particularly of concern in the elderly, who tend to take more drugs but metabolize them differently than the younger people usually repre-sented in drug-company studies. Anderson tells the story of an eighty-year-old man who had osteoarthritis and was given a drug that made him nauseated. His doctor pre-scribed an anti-nauseant, which, after several months, pro-duced a tremor. The man went to another doctor, who diagnosed Parkinson's disease and prescribed drugs to treat it, which increased the patient's nausea, resulting in an increase of anti-nausea drugs. Finally, a pharmacist had a conversation with the man's wife and recommended he be admitted to the hospital, where the drugs were carefully withdrawn. "He was discharged with a single prescription—Tylenol, for the osteoarthritis. Over the course of a year this man had become bedridden and now he was able to get back into life," says Anderson.

Discussions about the benefits and costs of various drugs often neglect the real-world consequences not only of known side effects but also of doctors' mistakes, patients' haphazard adherence to drug regimens, and unpredictable reactions. Most experts agree the toll is staggering. A 1998 analysis puts the annual death rate at 106,000, making adverse reactions to medication the fifth leading cause of death in the United States. Based on a conceptual model they developed, Bootman and a colleague estimate the cost of medication-related problems rivals that of cancer, Alzheimer's disease, and diabetes. In fact, according to this research, for each dollar we spend on medicines, we spend another dollar to treat new health problems caused by the medicines. "It happened in my family," says Bootman. "It happened to my grandmother. She got dizzy, fell down on our kitchen floor, broke her hip . . . It happens to people *all the time*."

As our society shifts toward taking more pharmaceuticals, more regularly, and for a wider array of reasons, there is, ironically, the potential to trivialize this important act, as if it were no more consequential than brushing one's teeth.

But if there's a proclivity in some quarters and in certain circumstances to blithely pill-swallow, in other cases people exhibit a deep resistance to taking medicine. This is particularly true of chronic-use medicines—things we're supposed to take every day for a long time, which includes some of the most important drugs to treat diabetes, heart disease, hypertension, and asthma, to name a few. "Patients only take about half the medication they should when it comes to chronic disease," says Joshua Benner, Pharm.D, Sc.D., who focuses on the issue as a researcher at Epinomics, a health-care research and consulting firm. They take the pills for a few months and then quit, or they stay on the regimen but frequently skip doses. This creates some of the medication-related illness Bootman talks about. It also generates waste; bottles sitting idle in medicine cabinets or pills taken every other day that should be taken daily don't repay the cost of their purchase with better health.

So why don't people take their medicine? Side effects and high cost—especially for people paying out of pocket—undoubtedly deter some. In a 2001 telephone survey by Harris Interactive, about one in seven adults said that during the last year they had taken a prescription drug in smaller doses than prescribed because of cost. About the same proportion said they had taken a drug less often than recommended to save money. Then there's the fact that often, chronic meds don't have observable effects. People stop taking antibiotics when they feel better. Asthmatics go for the "rescue" inhaler that opens their airways in a matter of moments, while neglecting the daily inhaler that could prevent wheezing in the first place. "It's a very complicated psychosocial issue," says Dennis Sprecher, MD, a specialist in preventive cardiology at the Cleveland Clinic. "Some people feel they're doing something very unnatural in taking pills. There are some who find it inconvenient. There are those who really don't internalize the need for some sort of treatment when they feel okay." In a study of medicines returned to Canadian pharmacies as part of a safe disposal program, researchers found that on average 60 percent of the original prescription was returned. Asked why they were tossing the medicine, 7 percent of patients said they simply didn't want to take it. The heart of the issue, says Sprecher, is that it's extremely tough to do anything on a routine basis, including beneficial habits like exercising and cooking healthy meals.

Take the cholesterol-lowering statins. The first statin, Mevacor, hit the market in the late 1980s, followed by five other products and increasing statin use during the 1990s. The news emerging from clinical trials of statins in the 1990s tells a tale quite different from the disappointments of HRT: Statins not only lower cholesterol, they prevent coronary events like heart attacks, and not only in people with established heart disease but also in those at increased risk for it. The National Cholesterol Education Program of the NIH recently updated guidelines for managing high cholesterol, bringing many more people into the definition of "high-risk." If put into practice, according to an estimate by IMS Health, these guidelines could nearly triple the number of people taking cholesterol-lowering drugs from 13 million to 36 million. The latest trial demonstrated benefits among people at high risk for coronary heart disease but with normal cholesterol. In reporting the results in 2001, Oxford University's Rory Collins, MD, said 200 million people worldwide were now eligible for statin use. "Even if an extra 10 million people took them, we would save 50,000 lives a year," he said. Statins, says Sprecher, are "an exciting new drug," a "dimensional leap" in the preventive treatment of cardiovascular disease.

Pharmaceutical companies have had little trouble selling a winner like this. In 2001, the number of U.S. statin prescriptions reached 110 million, making them the third-most-prescribed class after codeine preparations and anti-depressants, according to IMS Health. But according to an analysis by the market-research firm, in the last few years as market expansion slowed and competition among statin products heated up, the marketing cost to generate those new scripts also crept up. The promotional cost to spawn one new prescription, between $60 and $80 in 1997, rose to $120 or more in 1999. At one point in 2000, one company spent $800 to generate each new prescription. "With more players in the market for an extended period, the cost of share of voice to obtain new prescriptions increases," says a report of the IMS analysis in *Medical Marketing and Media*. "The cost of trying to catch up to the leader is very high." Under these competitive circumstances, companies are devoting their prodigious energies not only to growing the statin market in general but to proving that their statin is more potent, or safer, or better proven than somebody else's.

But such considerations are "noise," as Sprecher puts it, compared with the question of whether people are actually taking their medicine. To a surprising degree, they aren't. While at Harvard Medical School, Benner conducted a study among older patients who had been prescribed statin drugs and found that fewer than half lasted six months on the therapy. After five years, only one-fourth were still taking their meds regularly. "We found compliance is awful, even when the drug is free," he says. "We could only imagine it would be worse if you had to pay for it." In another study, 66 percent of patients prescribed statins at the Cleveland Clinic had less reduction in "bad" LDL cholesterol than the product's labeling would have predicted. Nearly one in five had no reduction in bad cholesterol.

The full promise of statins, especially to prevent first heart attacks or strokes, is predicated on people taking them rather more devotedly than they typically do. According to the U.S. Preventive Services Task Force, in a population comparable to those enrolled in statin primary-prevention trials, meaning those who are at increased risk but without established coronary disease, sixty-seven people would need to be treated for five years in order to prevent one cardiovascular event such as a heart attack.

No one has more to gain from patients finishing their meds and refilling their prescriptions than the pharmaceutical industry itself. And a small army of consultants has assembled to assist the industry in developing various behavior-modification programs to get people doing just that. Industry researchers are working on long-term dosing systems that would eliminate the need for pills, while small firms offer such devices as vibrating pendants and watches to remind patients when it's time for their medicine. In the meantime, both the industry and the medical community have proven themselves far more successful at spreading the word about statins—broadening recommendations for their use and generating new prescriptions—than they have at making sure that the people who need them most reap the drugs' full benefit by taking them every day, for years.

## ECONOMIES

As anyone who struggles to adopt healthy habits knows, there are only so many things we can focus on in a year, or do in a day. There are only so many medicines, vitamins, supplements, or other medical interventions our bodies can handle. And there are limits to what we are willing and able to spend. These realities point to the necessity of practicing certain economies when it comes to drugs. The pharmaceutical industry incurs "opportunity costs" when it sinks money into a particular R&D project, making the funds unavailable for investment elsewhere. But consumers incur such costs, too. When we decide which drugs to buy and use, we're implicitly choosing to forgo other medicines or health initiatives.

Drug industry boosters and, sometimes, proponents of insurance coverage for prescription drugs, argue that drugs are a good deal, that they save money while helping people live longer and healthier lives. But of course drugs are not all the same. Some medicines save money on other health-care costs; a relatively few save enough to make up for the cost of the drug itself. That's okay, because most people are happy to pay for better health. But now comes the nettlesome question: How much health for the money? Are medicines "cost effective"? That depends on how effective the individual drug is, its price, and, crucially, how it's used. "Blood pressure drugs are an excellent deal for diabetics. They are in fact cost-saving," says Louise Russell, Ph.D., an expert in cost-effectiveness analysis at Rutgers University's Institute for Health, Health Care Policy and Aging Research. "But the more you use the drug for people whose conditions are modest instead of severe or who are early in the process, often the less health benefit you get from it."

The question of whether a drug is cost effective for a health system is, of course, different from the questions an individual might ask when weighing the benefits and costs of taking a particular drug. How do you value Viagra for someone unable to make love? Immunization is very cost effective for society, but individuals sometimes forgo the shots and are not worse off for it. Still, measures of public and personal benefit overlap considerably. For starters, people like Melva McCuddy don't have the luxury of dismissing cost, since it'll come out of their personal budgets. In other cases, while the health system takes on the money cost of the drug, the patient takes on the inconvenience, side effects, and risks; if the potential benefit is small, it might not be worth it. Individuals and systems don't need *more* drugs or *fewer* drugs. We need the *right* drugs, for the right people.

"A lot of patients in my practice are on ten or eleven medications and I think I do a very good job of being parsimonious," says Steinman at the University of California at San Francisco. On the other hand, he says, sometimes with a new patient, "you pull out their medication list and you say, 'Oh my God, what *is* all that garbage?'"

For an individual, good sense might mean switching to a generic or over-the-counter form of one drug, but making sure not to skip doses of another medicine. Cheri Rockholdt Schmit, R.Ph., a pharmacist in Iowa, says she calls physicians probably three times a week to ask whether a patient really needs to be taking Celebrex, versus ibuprofen or naproxen, for pain. She carefully explains to elderly diabetics that the Glucophage XR many are taking is a once-a-day version of a drug they could get a lot cheaper in generic form. "Most of them are taking something else twice a day anyway," she says. She also follows up with patients to ask about side effects and to make sure they're refilling important prescriptions for managing their asthma, or blood pressure, or diabetes. "We try to keep patients' best interests in mind," says

Rockholdt Schmit. "In some cases it may be a matter of using the medication correctly or taking more of it, and in other cases it might be saying, you don't need all of this."

On a systemwide level, however we decide to apportion resources, practicing good sense requires a very sophisticated analysis of the good we're getting for the money we're spending. This means comparing, head to head, the effectiveness of various drugs and other interventions to treat a certain illness. It means cost-effectiveness research that looks at all the benefits—in terms of longevity and quality of life as well as dollar savings on hospitalizations and other care—and all the costs, including opportunity costs and the risk of side effects or drug-related illness.

But whom can we trust to answer these questions? What entity has a vested interest in the long-term health of Americans *and* in reasonable cost savings? As Russell points out, while Europeans tend to see cost-effectiveness considerations in medical care as a part of life to be gotten on with, Americans are highly suspicious of any attempts to limit treatment. This may reflect our intolerance for inaction (for God's sake *do* something), but it also stems from the fact that we can't assume the savings will be used to benefit us in some other way, or even to benefit some other consumer—say, to buy an elderly person a flu shot. Russell says, "We think, well, where is it going to go? The thought is, profits and insurance companies. If I forgo the Claritin, some insurance organization is going to make bigger profits, and I could care less." Should we trust these questions to drug companies? According to Patty Kumbera, an executive of Outcomes Pharmaceutical Health Care, the program in which pharmacist Rockholdt Schmit participates, drug companies have approached her about working together to promote specific products that happen to cut a good cost-benefits profile—but they want nothing to do with the part of the program that steers patients away from waste.

When it comes to decisions about who uses which drugs, Americans are caught between powerful, profit-driven forces. On one hand, the insurers who pay for care do well when they spend less money. Theoretically they're motivated to spend on drugs or other initiatives that save money by improving health in the long run; as a practical matter, they generally don't cover the same people over a lifetime, so they can't depend on reaping the rewards of early investment in long-term health. Pharmaceutical companies—the source of medicines, but also of information about medicines—have a stake in selling product. A drugmaker benefits when its drug is used for more indications, over a longer period of time, by the young as well as the old, the relatively healthy as well as the very sick. These forces may not always behave according to the incentives upon which they're based, but in the aggregate they do.

So the drug industry cries, "Access!" and the insurance industry cries, "Waste!" Researchers at the Harvard School of Public Health recently compared cost-effectiveness studies according to who had paid for the research. On average, those funded by the drug industry reported by far the best cost-effectiveness ratios; those funded by health-care organizations reported by far the worst. Unfortunately, such research is too complex to simply split the difference. Likewise, there are reams of data comparing the efficacy of particular drugs to placebo, but few that compare them with each other. Meanwhile, there are thousands of evidence-based practice guidelines telling physicians the best way to treat particular illnesses. They come from specialty physician groups, various government entities, various advocacy groups—very useful, yes, but it's sometimes hard for doctors and consumers to keep track of them, much less judge which are most credible.

The upshot: American consumers, so intent on the primacy of the doctor-patient relationship and the individual's right to make health-care decisions, are awash in data, offered guidance at every turn, inundated by commercial messages. But we are oddly impoverished in the way of unbiased, approachable information about the usefulness and cost of one drug versus another.

Many have called for the establishment of some central organization to study medicines, their relative effectiveness, and, at least by implication, cost effectiveness. In some countries, England and Australia, for example, the government plays this role, but in the United States—partly because of the fortunes that stand to be lost or made—government dissemination of health-care guidelines has proven intensely controversial and politically dangerous. In the early 1990s, the federal Agency for Health Care Policy and Research led the way in producing evidence-based guidelines for clinical practice, gathering experts together to perform the most sophisticated statistical analyses. "Industry representatives were critical, there were lawsuits filed, it was quite a scene," recalls Stephen Woolf, MD, a professor of family practice at Virginia Commonwealth University who has served on the U.S. Preventive Services Task Force, a panel of experts assembled by the government to review preventive strategies. Contentious as the guidelines were in general, it was a 1995 guideline for the management of low back pain—which did not support surgery—that erupted in the most furious controversy. Economist Reinhardt, who was involved in lobbying to save the agency, says, "*One* orthopedic surgeon got to *one* Congressman and almost killed the entire agency. We came to the rescue and said, 'All right all right, we won't do guidelines.'" The agency was soon renamed the Agency for Healthcare Research and Quality. Instead of issuing guidelines, it sponsors detailed reviews of various treatments by twelve academic "evidence-based practice centers." These evidence reviews are then turned over to partner organizations such as professional societies, which can use them to produce their own guidelines.

Reinhardt believes that we Americans will never get control of drug spending until we "shore up the demand side"—that is, get smart about the drugs we buy. But to do that, we need unbiased evaluation of the products on offer. To this end Reinhardt suggests the government launch a set of drug-research centers that would operate as independent nonprofits, recruiting the best researchers to tell us the truth about pharmaceutical products—their benefits and costs—starting with the most prescribed, most expensive ones. Such research could form a rational basis for health insurers' coverage decisions, a basis that patients might actually trust. "The things that I propose, an endowment of independent research organizations that can really do drug research—how could you argue with that?" asks Reinhardt. But he predicts with equal conviction that nothing of the sort will come to pass: "The industry," he says, "would never allow it to happen."

# chapter 7

# NOTHIN'S GONNA CHANGE MY WORLD

DRUGMAKERS didn't make the world. They didn't dream up the system in which some Americans are represented in pricing negotiations while others are left to fend for themselves. It's not their fault that so many—from doctors to patient-advocacy groups to universities to movie stars—have become reliant on their information, not to mention their money. No drug-company executive engineered the medical-care apparatus that lets patients be squeezed between the opposing financial interests of those who sell and those who pay.

Big pharmaceutical companies didn't create this system, not single-handedly, but, boy, do they know how to defend it. If the drug industry exerts its influence in our homes, in doctor's offices and hospitals, in the halls of academia, and on the pages of learned journals, nowhere is it more powerful than in Washington, D.C. Among critics of the industry, any discussion about why things are the way they are eventually comes around to the men and women of the drug lobby. It is established, it is sophisticated—and even in the terms of modern politics, it is colossal.

Public Citizen combed through lobbying records submitted to the federal government during the 1999–2000 election cycle, a critical one for drug companies, with a Medicare drug benefit up for grabs. What emerges from the group's extensive database is the portrait of a lobbying force 625 members strong—bigger than Congress itself. Drug companies spent more money to influence politicians than did insurance companies, telephone companies, electric companies, commercial banks, oil and gas producers, automakers, tobacco companies, and food processors and manufacturers, more, in short, than any other industry. Most of that—about $177 million—went to hire lobbyists from 134 firms, including twenty-one former members of Congress. The industry also gave $20 million in campaign contributions and spent $60 million on issue ads.

According to another group, the Center for Responsive Politics, the drug industry ranked number twelve among more than eighty industries in campaign contributions in the last election cycle; in 2001–2002, it was number nine in political gifts. Whereas a decade ago contributions were split pretty evenly among Republicans and Democrats, the industry is increasingly throwing in its lot with the Republican party, with three out of four dollars going to Republicans. This bet paid off in 2000 and again in 2002, sealing a mutually advantageous relationship between the drug industry and the party in power.

If the drug lobby has gone on high alert in recent years, it's for good reason. With drug costs spiraling, insurers, employers, unions, consumer groups, and the public at large, especially politically organized seniors, are pressing Congress to act. Once quite positive, public opinion about the drug industry dipped rather precipitously after 1997, according to a Kaiser Family Foundation–Harvard School of Public Health survey; by 2000, the last year of the survey, fewer than half of respondents rated the industry as doing a good job "serving health care consumers."

So far, though, the industry has managed to turn back just about every attempt to rein in drug costs and threaten its growth spurt. Some drug-industry critics, like Sager, predict a backlash: "They're playing out a losing endgame," he says. "The sooner they compromise, the better the chances they will emerge with their profits and reputations intact. If they don't compromise they will succeed in electing the world's angriest Congress." Others, like Wennar, express frustration over the stalemate in Washington and the industry's stubborn defense of the status quo. "We are firm supporters of a prescription drug benefit under Medicare," she says in monotone, imitating the industry's repeated assurances on this score. "Don't even bother to show up," she says. "Just send a CD with it playing."

Adding a drug benefit to Medicare has, indeed, become the fulcrum of the debate. Public Citizen's investigation found that industry lobbyists spent a great deal of time in 1999–2000 on pricing issues, resisting drug-reimportation legislation as well as efforts to reform the pediatric-research incentive. But the industry's most intensive lobbying was aimed at influencing the outcome on Medicare. A Medicare drug benefit could be enormously profitable for the drug industry—*if* it boosts volume without containing prices.

In recent plans, Senate Democrats propose pumping

roughly $425 billion into prescription drugs for Medicare over eight years, versus $310 billion over ten years for the House Republican plan. But there's a key difference in the way the plans are structured. In the Republican approach, Medicare enrollees would purchase government-subsidized pharmaceutical coverage through competing private insurance plans that could vary actual benefits and costs. The Democratic plan would offer a single drug-benefits structure for Medicare, in effect creating a new government customer with the muscle—if not the explicit mandate—to exert downward pressure on prices. The latter is exactly what drugmakers most fervently wish to avoid, fighting it off with rhetoric that raises the specter of seniors losing "access" and "choice" in a "one-size-fits-all big government program."

The drug industry's political exertions over the last few years, including political ads aimed at key congressional candidates, helped prepare the way for the narrow passage in the House in June 2002 of the GOP version of a Medicare drug benefit. In a particularly bold display of industry insiderism, pharmaceutical companies were among the top donors at a lavish GOP fund-raiser two days after the drug-benefit plan's unveiling—and two days before its passage. The *Washington Post* reported that GlaxoSmithKline's chief operating officer was the head corporate fund-raiser for the event, with GSK contributing at least $250,000. Other big donors included PhRMA, Pfizer, Eli Lilly, Bayer AG, and Merck.

Deep ideological differences made it unlikely Congress would clinch Medicare prescription-drug coverage in 2002, and in fact, the Republican version died in the Senate. But some pols refused to let up on reimportation and a bill to reform Hatch-Waxman. On the generic drugs legislation, an array of political-interest groups fanned out to oppose the drug lobby: consumer groups, insurance companies, employers, unions. "It's pretty much every segment of Washington lobbying, minus PhRMA," says one Senate staffer. "But PhRMA's still on top. They've got so many more people and so much more money and that just buys a lot of access. Instead of being able to go out and educate people on our bill, we're constantly on the defensive, because PhRMA got there first."

Indeed, on generic drugs, Big Pharma finds itself facing off against traditional allies, pals even, fellow members of the National Association of Manufacturers or the U.S. Chamber of Commerce who've fought shoulder to shoulder with drugmakers on other issues but are fed up with increases in drug spending for their employee health plans. By some accounts, the debate has turned just a little bit ugly. "They think it's their life's blood," says one industry lobbyist who supports legislation that would sharply limit drugmakers' access to the thirty-month stay to protect patented medicines against generic competition. "In some cases they have taken it very personally. To the extent of calling a couple of the lobbyists' bosses back at headquarters, saying that we didn't understand the issue, that we were out over our skis," he says with indignation. In one meeting of manufacturing-industry representatives, says the lobbyist, pharma reps turned to their colleagues with a plea for unity: "They said, 'We're the new Marlboro Man. You need to help us not have that image.' And we basically said, 'It's not our fault that you have that public-relations problem. You need to fix

it on your own.'" Still, several major corporations have
dropped out of Business for Affordable Medicine (BAM), a
coalition formed to press for generics legislation; according
to Hill staffers, at least one did so because drugmakers
hinted that they would cancel important business with
BAM members. Meanwhile, in publications that circulate
on the Hill, PhRMA has run bare-knuckle ads against the
generics legislation. "Pray for a Miracle," says an ad in *Congress Daily,* showing a pallid, slight child with a kerchief tied
over her apparently bald head, "Because Generic Drugs Will
Never Cure Her."

Out among the folks, the pharmaceutical lobby is too
savvy to let itself appear like just another bunch of black
hats looking to protect a profitable concern. In much the
same way it portrays its research as principally a means to
banish suffering and its advertising as public-health education, the drug industry has sought to cloak its self-inter-
ested political activism in the garments of populist foment.
In a 1999 ad campaign attacking the Clinton Medicare benefit plan, it wasn't a pharmaceutical executive but "Flo"
who addressed the American public. An older woman in
bowling garb, Flo told viewers that in order to "guarantee
research for tomorrow's cures," they should support "the
right Medicare reforms." "I don't want big government in
my medicine cabinet!" she famously exclaimed. The ads
announced that they were paid for by Citizens for Better
Medicare (CBM) but didn't mention that the group gets
the great majority of its funding from pharmaceutical companies or that its director had recently moved from his post
as PhRMA's advertising chief. Later, Citizens for Better
Medicare ran ads in various markets criticizing the Cana-

dian health-care system and attacking Democratic candidates for "playing politics" by leading bus trips or issuing reports on price differences between the United States and Canada. In all, CBM was responsible for more than one-fourth of all "issue" ads from nonparty sources in the critical months leading up to the 2000 election, Public Citizen reports.

Today, CBM's web site describes the group as a "grassroots" coalition to which members contribute "time, energy and effort," though "most of our funding is provided by contributions from America's pharmaceutical research companies." For months, a link promising to introduce browsers to activists for Citizens for Better Medicare has pulled up the message, "Coming soon." In the meantime, browsers are invited to send a form e-mail to friends: "Will seniors be forced into a huge government-run program to get the medicines they need? . . . Will they have the same kind of choices and access when big government reaches into their medicine cabinets?"

In the run-up to the 2002 election, PhRMA used grants to a conservative seniors organization to subsidize another multimillion-dollar television ad blitz praising mostly Republican candidates for supporting "real prescription drug coverage" through Medicare—meaning the market-based GOP version the drugmakers favor. The ads, announced as "paid for by United Seniors Association," featured avuncular television star Art Linkletter. PhRMA's role in the campaign remained under the radar.

The drug industry has also taken its "grassroots" organizing to the states, where legislatures have been shifting their emphasis from subsidizing drug costs for the poor to containing those costs. Last year alone more than twenty states have considered legislation to allow state governments to negotiate with drug manufacturers for supplemental rebates to state Medicaid programs. Some state initiatives would extend negotiated benefits to state residents without insurance, while others have instituted formularies for Medicaid beneficiaries. According to the progressive Center for Policy Alternatives (CPA), which has produced model state drug-pricing legislation, the drug industry has launched phony citizen campaigns to defeat such measures in Maryland, Florida, Georgia, Indiana, Minnesota, New Mexico, North Carolina, Virginia, and Washington state.

The efforts are coordinated by Washington PR firm Bonner & Associates, well known for what activists call "Astro-turf" (as opposed to the real stuff) lobbying. Telemarketers at Bonner call local residents or organizations and, presenting themselves as advocates for seniors or the poor, ask them to contact their legislature or sign a resolution against the drug-pricing measure. "They say, 'Hi, I'm from the Indiana Consumer Alliance,'" says CPA policy director Bernie Horn. "They're sitting at 17th and L saying this. There is no Indiana Consumer Alliance." Although this approach isn't unique to the drug industry, it's unusual for it to be employed at the state level, says Horn. "These are congressional tactics," he says, "but the big fight's in the states—they've won on the federal level."

In 2000 in the state of Maine, the industry's best efforts to defeat a first-of-its kind drug-pricing measure were defeated. The Maine Rx law allows the state to bring to all uninsured residents the same discounts Medicaid gets for drugs. "When we lobbied for the bill, we were at the statehouse for two months," says union rep and Rx activist Vi Quirion. "We were there until midnight." As for the other side, it was a running joke among proponents of the law that at the very least, their efforts would give Augusta a shot in the arm by attracting lobbyists to its hotels and restaurants. "Oh my god, there were so many of them," says Quirion.

But the law and others like it face legal challenges from the industry. Courts struck down a Vermont drug-pricing measure in 2001. And in July 2002, PhRMA filed an important lawsuit against the federal government, saying it has no authority to allow a formulary-based Medicaid price-control measure in Michigan—or, ultimately, in any state. According to the *Wall Street Journal*, the Michigan law, which creates a list of "preferred" drugs for state Medicaid beneficiaries, quickly induced two drugmakers to sharply reduce prices in order to maintain market share. Pfizer took another approach, asking patients who'd been switched to a new drug under the program to call a toll-free number to report their experiences, which were distributed to state lawmakers. The *Journal* called some of these testimonials "chilling." And yet it seems worth noting that the drug industry has not been a vocal defender of patients subjected to drug switching by PBMs.

As for Maine Rx, states intent on emulating Maine await the outcome of PhRMA's legal challenge, which has blocked implementation of the law. A federal judge ruled against Maine Rx soon after its passage. That decision was overturned on appeal. But the U.S. Supreme Court accepted PhRMA's appeal and began hearing arguments in January 2003. The trade group argues, among other things, that Maine Rx runs afoul of federal law by predicating Medicaid coverage for given drugs on drugmakers' willingness to give discounts on those drugs to other uninsured citizens. "This case is about whether Maine can deprive Medicaid patients of the medicines they need for reasons unrelated to Medicaid," Marjorie Powell, PhRMA's senior assistant general counsel, said in a prepared statement inaugurating the Supreme Court case. She called the law "a blow to Maine's neediest patients."

Meanwhile Vi Quirion, though she has appeared in political ads supporting the (failed) U.S. Senate campaign of Maine Rx architect Chellie Pingree, is no actress. For forty-four years she worked in the Hathaway shirt factory. Unlike "Flo," she really is a Medicare beneficiary; moreover, she is ill. In the last few years, as Congress engaged the drug lobby's onslaught and courts considered the constitutionality of Maine Rx, Quirion underwent cancer surgery and a knee replacement. Between antibiotics for complications from the knee surgery and drugs to prevent cancer recurrence, Quirion has been hard pressed to meet her own prescription-drug bills. One month, after paying $345 for a prescription, she had only $100 left for food and other day-to-day expenses. Her arduous trips to Canada are no stunt. When Maine Rx is rolled out, she says, "we won't have to go anymore, because we're going to negotiate for better prices just like some of the other countries."

# chapter 8

# THE GOOSE THAT LAID THE GOLDEN EGG

IN 1849, GERMAN-BORN cousins Charles Pfizer and Charles Erhart launched a small chemicals operation in Brooklyn, New York; its first product mixed santonin, a terribly bitter plant extract used to kill intestinal worms, with a toffee flavoring that made it palatable. Down the road in Philadelphia, brothers John and Frank Wyeth opened a modest drugstore in 1860. Nearly thirty years later in an apartment on Chicago's North Side, Dr. Wallace Abbott perfected his method for producing tiny pills that delivered standard doses of various medicinal plants. By the turn of the century, Merck, with beginnings as a pharmacy in Darmstadt, Germany, was producing 10,000 chemicals and ready-to-use medicines and had branches in London, New York, and Moscow.

In the last 150 years, medicine makers have evolved from local druggists or chemical makers to mid-sized manufacturing operations with regional distribution to very large research-based companies whose reach is truly global.

Americans have greeted each new wave of products, from elixirs for colds to antibiotics to drugs that prevent brain damage during a stroke, with awe and gratitude. But Americans' relationship with the industry has also been punctuated by crises of confidence, periods when government, media, and consumers turned on their goose-that-laid-the-golden-egg with resentment and suspicion. Were the new medicines really safe? Were we being told the truth about them? Were we being manipulated by the industry's marketing and exploited by its pricing? In answering these questions, Americans have taken bold steps—often leading the world, and sometimes over industry objections—to ensure that their medicines are safe, effective, unadulterated, and accurately labeled. But our grapplings with the economics of the drug industry—with the goose itself—have proven more frustrating. While Europeans and others have felt perfectly comfortable domesticating the creature, pressing it into the service of public health, Americans, devoted to the notion that in seeking its own good it will further our own, have seen fit to let the goose run wild.

One of the first crises of public confidence came in the latter part of the nineteenth century. With the rise of communications and advertising in America came a panoply of tonics and elixirs promising the folks relief from what ailed them. These so-called patent medicines ran the gamut from common laxatives to morphine- and booze-spiked preparations for fussy babies to putative cures for cancer; their ingredients were proprietary, secret. Drugmakers wishing to differentiate themselves from the peddlers of mythical potions dubbed their own products "ethical" pharmaceuticals, emphasizing the purity and not the secrecy of their products—which generally weren't patented—and advertising and selling their drugs to doctors and druggists, not to the public. In 1905, the weekly magazine *Collier's* published a series, "The Great American Fraud," condemning patent medicines as worthless and dangerous, "palatable poison for the poor." Ethical drugmakers supported the passage in 1906 of the Pure Food and Drug Act, which forbade interstate commerce in food and drugs whose labels did not accurately reflect their ingredients.

The ethical drugmakers proceeded over the next decades to draw closer to science, hiring research personnel mainly to establish manufacturing techniques that would enable them to produce medicines in quantity, achieve standardization of strength and dosage, and meet expectations for purity. In the early part of the twentieth century, pharmaceutical houses offered similar lines of common medicines, relying on their catalogues' range and reputation for quality to attract customers. Promotions encouraged doctors to "Ask for Mulford's" or "Always specify Parke Davis," according to a history of the industry's early development, *Medical Science and Medical Industry* by Jonathan Liebenau, Ph.D. The companies' laboratories came up with new drugs, but often they used existing ingredients. "[I]t took relatively little effort to devise a useful amalgam of standard preparations to combine, for example, a temperature-reducing drug with a stomach-soothing agent," writes Liebenau.

Another major crisis came in the 1930s, when the S.E. Massengill Company produced a liquid form of a new antibacterial, sulfanilamide, that killed more than a hundred people, mostly children. The company had mixed the active ingredient with a toxic solvent. The scandal was widely reported and raised public alarm over the safety of drugs, leading to the quick adoption of drug regulation whose merits had been debated for years. The Federal Food, Drug, and Cosmetic Act of 1938 required not only that ingredients of a drug be truthfully represented but that their safety be demonstrated by research before marketing.

Then came World War II, a watershed event for the pharmaceutical industry in America. Domestic companies were motivated to wean themselves from a long-standing dependence on innovation from Germany, where drugmakers had been in the habit of patenting their work. At the same time, the case of penicillin vividly illustrated what could be accomplished through systematic efforts at drug development. British scientists had identified the bacteria-killing potential of a common airborne mold and isolated enough of it to show it could kill infection in animals. In 1941, the federal government asked a handful of American drug companies to go hammer and tongs at the difficult problem of mass production. At the beginning of the war, there was barely enough penicillin for scientists to study it, but after the government authorized more than a dozen companies to manufacture it using a fermentation method devised by Pfizer, penicillin was rushed to battle zones in sufficient quantities to meet demand and save many lives.

After the war, companies started investing more in research and patenting their inventions. According to a Pfizer company history, then chief John L. Smith, on his deathbed in 1950, advised his successor not to relinquish proprietary rights to the raw materials it manufactured: "If anything comes out of this antibiotic soil-screening program, don't make the mistake we made with penicillin and hand it over to other companies. Let's sell it ourselves. Go into the pharmaceutical business if we have to." In the years that followed, drug companies brought a panoply of breakthrough medicines, "wonder drugs" as they were known to a generation, to market: antibiotics, oral diabetes medicines, antihypertensives, antihistamines, and tranquilizers, to name a few. "With patent protection they could charge relatively high prices," says Scherer, the Harvard economist, who as a young research assistant in the 1950s helped represent Pfizer in a federal antitrust case involving the new antibiotic tetracycline. "In the case of tetracycline, it cost somewhere between $2 and $4 to produce 100 capsules. The price to retail druggists was $31 roughly. That was the first big breakthrough, and they realized that in discovering these unique and patentable molecules was gold." During the 1940s, 192 new chemical entities—drugs using new ingredients—were introduced in the United States. In the 1950s, the number rose to 453.

The pace of new drug introductions precipitated the rise of the "detail man." As a practical matter, no institution outside the drug companies was prepared to send representatives to personally explain to doctors the new products' mechanisms and indications. But the goal of the detail man was also to establish and reinforce brand-name loyalty. The big drug houses, in addition to selling patented products unique to one company, also sold what we now think of as generics, but under different brand names. Sometimes, these were unpatented products; other times, the patent holder licensed sales rights to other companies. The tranquilizer meprobamate was sold by Carter Products as Miltown and by Wyeth Laboratories as Equanil. Tetracycline was

sold by different houses as Tetracyn, Achromycin, Polycy-
cline, Steclin, and Panmycin. One commentator described
the situation for doctors as being akin to grocery shoppers
having to look for beans under labels like "Nabes," "Sne-
abs," "Lo-cals," and "Hi-pros." The proliferation of brand
names and the accompanying risk of counterfeiting led to
the establishment during the 1950s and 1960s of laws that
required all prescriptions to be filled as written. Thus, if a
detail man could fix his company's brand name in doctors'
minds, that brand would outsell the competition—including
much cheaper equivalents sold under generic names by
smaller firms—well after patent expiration. A detail man for
Lederle was quoted in a 1958 Federal Trade Commission
report, "[The company] was interested in bombarding
physicians with the Achromycin name and we did just
that and got the name across. We swamped them with
Achromycin."

This "develop, patent, promote" strategy reduced the
generics business to a state of quiescence. In 1948, 40 percent of U.S. prescriptions were written generically; by 1965,
only 5 percent of prescriptions came without a brand name.

The 1950s saw the establishment of the drug industry as
we know it—characterized by heavy investment in research
and promotion, high prices, and high profitability. This
period of rapid growth for the industry also led to a parox-
ysm of public scrutiny that in almost every particular prefig-
ures criticisms levied against the industry by politicians and
consumer groups today. In 1959, Senator Estes Kefauver, a
Democrat from Tennessee, opened a series of broad-ranging
hearings on drug-industry operations, calling innumerable
witnesses and producing many hundreds of pages of tran-

scripts. The senator and his colleagues accused the drug-makers of exploiting the sick with excessive markups over the cost of production, charging lower prices abroad and to powerful customers like hospitals, and engaging in various forms of competition that did not involve lowering prices, including intensive advertising and manipulating molecules to produce "me-too" drugs.

The hearings were enlivened by such colorful moments as when Dr. James E. Bowes of Salt Lake City testified that he had weighed the drug-company mail arriving at his office and calculated that the amount of such mail going to American physicians equaled well over 24,000 tons a year. Said Dr. Bowes, "[I]t would take over 25 trash trucks to haul it away, to be burned on a dump pile whose blaze would be seen for 50 miles around." Less amusing were the letters the committee received from elderly people with arthritis who, living on $60 a month from Social Security, were going without food to buy brand-name Meticorten at $30 a month, even though generic cortisones were available for $3 a month. Schering, the drug's maker—like other drugmakers testifying before the Senate committee, like drugmakers today—argued that its research expenses justified the markup on Meticorten. In his book *In a Few Hands: Monopoly Power in America*, Kefauver countered that taking into account the research expenses the drugmaker reported to the committee, the ratio of production costs to price for Meticorten would be one and one-half cents to sixteen and one-half cents, as opposed to one and one-half cents to eighteen cents. The bigger issue, wrote Kefauver, was advertising. "Schering was in the enviable position of being able to spend lavish sums on promotion because of its high profits, and then to perpetuate these high profits because its heavy promotional campaigns to physicians increased prescriptions of Schering's brand-name products," he wrote.

Kefauver's hearings, although embarrassing to the drug industry, appeared to be going nowhere politically—until the issue of safety once again burst onto the scene in the form of a human tragedy that overnight turned calls for legislative reform into public and political conviction. The name of the drug lives in infamy: thalidomide. Popular as a sleeping pill and treatment for morning sickness in Germany and a few other countries, thalidomide had not yet received FDA clearance for marketing in the United States when news emerged that it had caused terrible birth defects in hundreds of babies. The American company set to sell the drug as Kevadon in the United States withdrew its FDA application; but 20,000 patients had already been treated in a prelaunch clinical trial whose purpose seemed to have more to do with marketing the drug than studying it. The company had advised its salespeople to, among other things, "[a]ppeal to the doctor's ego—we think he is important enough to be selected as one of the first to use Kevadon in that section of the country."

At this juncture, the drug industry could not escape a massive regulatory overhaul in America, one that was soon emulated by other developed nations. But the Kefauver-Harris Drug Amendments of 1962 did not reflect the senator's passionate interest in reforming the economics of the drug industry. He had wanted to get a firm grasp of the goose itself, for example, to require drug patent holders to license their products to other companies after three years, in exchange for a royalty of up to 8 percent of sales. Instead, the amendments essentially extended the consumer's right to assurances as to the goose's product—the drug supply. Still, they extended this right in critical ways, giving the FDA oversight of premarketing clinical trials and establishing requirements for "fair balance" between risks and benefits in drug advertising. Most important, the new laws for the first time required drug companies to demonstrate not only their products' safety but also their effectiveness. This made it far more complicated and expensive to get a drug approved for sale in the United States. The industry howled. In a long interview conducted as part of an FDA oral history project, FDA lawyer William W. Goodrich, who served between 1939 and 1971, recalls that the commissioner at the time of the Kefauver amendments "got an awful lot of static" about his failure to follow through expeditiously with regulations based on the legislation. "[W]e had our hands full with litigation with the drug industry about the regulations, and that was what was holding things up," he said.

Nevertheless, during the 1960s the FDA undertook an extraordinary process, one that would be politically unthinkable today: While defending its regulations in court, it assigned the National Academy of Sciences to review the efficacy of products approved since 1938—and yanked drugs that didn't meet the test. By 1984, of 3,443 products acted on by the FDA, nearly one-third, or 1,051 in all, had been found not effective. And in 1970, the Court of Appeals ruled against the industry in the landmark case of *Upjohn v. Finch:* No, said the court, commercial success did not constitute proof of efficacy. In spite of drugmakers' resistance, the efficacy requirement may ultimately have benefited them, for now any new drug product that came on the market bore the federal government's implicit endorsement as both safe and useful; it *worked*. Moreover, the very high expense of getting past the FDA to the promised land of the American market, a hurdle for the big houses, was even more formidable for upstarts. The new rules "radically changed the environment for testing," says Scherer. "The industry bemoaned it, but realized that in the end it hasn't hurt them because it raises the ticket to entry such that relatively few need apply or dare apply."

Let the good times roll. Despite sharply increased generic competition resulting from the repeal of antisubstitution laws in the 1970s, and later Hatch-Waxman; despite the growth of insurance organizations with the muscle to negotiate better prices; despite increasing research costs, the 1980s and 1990s have been a period of robust revenue growth for Big Pharma. Double-digit increases in U.S. prices were, according to one writer in *Pharmaceutical Marketing in the Twenty-first Century*, "the ultimate lever of global profitability during the 1980s," followed by somewhat more modest increases in prices and large boosts in volume during the 1990s. Perhaps related to both price and volume trends is the fact that during these years, thanks to the rise of managed-care insurance, consumers have had to pay less and less out of their own pockets for drugs. In 1990, nearly half of all prescription-drug spending was paid for directly by consumers, but by 1998, that figure had dropped to 27 percent. During the Kefauver hearings, it was remarked that "the man who orders" (the doctor) doesn't pay, and "the man who pays" (the patient) doesn't order, distorting the usual rules of consumer response to pricing. At the time, pretty much everyone was a cash-paying customer. These days, the person who takes the drug neither has the power to order it nor is likely to pay for it, at least not directly. Although millions like Melva McCuddy are excluded from its benefits, insurance coverage has given other consumers more access to prescription drugs, while making them less sensitive to high prices.

## BIG AND BIGGER

Perhaps the most important feeder of Big Pharma's growth has been a sea change within the drugs business itself. Since the inception of the modern pharmaceutical industry, and especially in the waning years of the twentieth century, large drug companies have shifted their emphasis from producing a broad range of products and competing in numerous therapeutic classes to cashing in on a few high-margin products with huge markets. Blockbusters. Claritin, Lipitor, Viagra, Prilosec, Celebrex, and Vioxx—these and other products worth $500 million or more in annual sales account for over 50 percent of total drug sales in the United States, up from 28 percent for the year ending July 1997, according to IMS Health.

In sales dollars, today's biggest blockbusters dwarf even the star products of yesteryear. During the late 1960s the relatively low-priced tranquilizer Valium, at one time the best-selling drug ever, lifted Swiss pharma company Roche to the top spot in the world pharmaceutical market, with over $750 million in company sales. At its peak, $4-a-pill Prilosec pulled in more than $4 billion in the United States alone, even accounting for general inflation and population growth, a horse of a different color. To build a blockbuster requires a massive concentration of resources; sampling, detailing, advertising, and perhaps postmarketing research are all brought to bear on targeted brands. "It used to be more of a natural evolution," says Ehrlich of Rx Insight. "Drug companies used to be more patient in watching a drug grow, and they would allow the doctor more time to adopt and use the drug. Slow build was accepted as a business goal." These days, in order to maximize the return on very substantial investments, a blockbuster's "rollout" has to be speedy, garnering big-figure sales in the first year or even six months. The marketing focus may then be sustained for months or years.

Leaving aside for the moment whether any of this makes sense for public health, some have questioned whether it's a sustainable gambit for the drug business. A single patent expiration can gut a multibillion-dollar blockbuster—and in so doing take a big chunk out of a company that's been in business for generations. "The sales and earnings growth of those old firms was 10 percent a year, forever, which was pretty good considering that they got through wars and depressions and so forth," says Art Hilgart, a former executive who spent thirty-three years with a top drugmaker. "When they changed their focus to blockbusters with extremely high markups, it meant steeper growth and higher earnings, but it also increased the pressure to get new products."

The cycle goes something like this: The more a company invests in promoting a single brand, the more trouble it's in when the brand goes off-patent and the more vigorously it will strive to (1) extend that brand's franchise, or (2) whip up demand for a new high-margin drug to replace lost revenue from the first, or both.

"[T]he industry has focused on building these megabrands, mainly marketed to general practitioners. The goal has been to build these products to as large as they can," Arnold H. Snider, who manages a $1.5 billion health-care stocks fund, recently told *Barron's*. Adding "We're saturating the doc. And after you finish promoting to the doc, you promote to the consumer. One of the problems they're having is that you build up such a critical mass in a few brands, when they go off-patent it's very difficult to replace them."

Indeed, the hunger for blockbusters is fed by Wall Street, tied to analysts' expectations for steady and steep earnings growth and their increasing proclivity to trawl company pipelines for portents of boom and bust. Ehrlich explains, "Wall Street analysts are excited by blockbusters, that's what they talk about, and therefore CEOs want blockbusters." Meanwhile, especially given patent expirations, it might be perfectly natural for a drugmaker's earnings to be "sawtoothed," as Hilgart puts it—higher one year, a bit lower the next. For an industry predicated on long-term investment in research, the yoking of a corporation's welfare to today's accounts receivable seems wrongheaded. "This narrow concentration on the present is ludicrous," says Hilgart. "If Lilly's Prozac suffers, its earnings are going to be down—but that doesn't mean that Lilly's prospects in the long run are weaker at all. Lilly's been growing for a hundred years."

The drugmakers' hunt for the biggest game has contributed to an extraordinary wave of mergers in the industry, creating team-ups that leave the pharmaceuticals field dominated by a few very big dogs. In 1999, Astra AB and Zeneca formed AstraZeneca, while Hoecht Marion Roussel and Rhone-Poulenc Rorer united as Aventis. In 2000, Glaxo Wellcome and SmithKline Beecham formed GlaxoSmith Kline; Pfizer took over Warner-Lambert; and Pharmacia & Upjohn joined Searle to become Pharmacia. These five companies accounted for more than one-third of all spending on drug promotions and nearly as big a portion of drug sales in 2000, according to a study by the Institute for Health and Socio-Economic Policy. Shortly after its acquisition of Warner-Lambert, Pfizer CEO William Steere told *Business Week*: "If Warner-Lambert did not have Lipitor [the blockbuster cholesterol-reducing drug], we would not have done this." In July 2002, Pfizer announced that it would also subsume rival Pharmacia, along with its several top-sellers, including big-winner Celebrex.

Getting bigger may tend to stifle competition in the long run because instead of having competing drugs to fill a certain niche, you'll have only one, but it doesn't necessarily relieve the pressure to replace revenues when a drug like Lipitor finally gives up to generic competition. According to NIHCM, in 2001 the five biggest drugmakers garnered from 48 percent to a full 80 percent of their sales from blockbusters with at least $1 billion in sales.

*Barron's* reported in May 2002 that GlaxoSmithKline, notwithstanding its colossal girth, "is clearly worried" about the possibility of generic competition to a few key products. The company conditioned earnings projections on winning patent challenges for Paxil and another drug—if not, says *Barron's*, "Glaxo might have to seek another merger." The investor's weekly pegged as a potential target ailing Bristol-

Myers Squibb, which itself is suffering from the loss of patent protection for the diabetes drug Glucophage. Glucophage was so critical to BMS that it lobbied Congress in an attempt (this time unsuccessful) to get three years' market exclusivity for pediatric labeling on the drug—over and above the six months' extra patent protection it had already received for running the pediatric trials. In the last years of Prozac's patent, Eli Lilly scrambled to get patients on new versions of the *Wunderdrug*—even, plaintiffs claim in an ongoing Florida lawsuit, mailing its once-a-week formulation of the pill directly to a few patients' homes (a claim the company has pledged to investigate). But Lilly's efforts to save its franchise have been mostly unavailing.

Over the next five years, many billions of dollars' worth of these top-sellers are scheduled to come off patent. Consumers can expect savings from generics, accompanied by a *very* intense sales pitch for Big Pharma's new line of patented products.

But the industry is facing pressure from other quarters, too. Its current modus operandi has led to the most dramatic failure of public confidence in our golden goose since thalidomide and the Kefauver hearings. This is especially so because widespread criticism of the industry a decade ago did little to change its direction. In 1989, Arkansas Democratic senator David Pryor led the Special Committee on Aging in a round of hearings to probe industry marketing excesses, discriminatory pricing, and, most of all, galloping price increases of the previous decade. During the 1980s, drug prices had risen 152 percent, with several major companies reneging on public promises to contain price hikes. In a searing letter introducing a 1991 committee report, Pryor wrote, "It was the hope of many in the Congress that the 1990 enactment of a Medicaid drug rebate law, which will provide modest cost relief to the program that serves the sickest and poorest of our poor, coupled with the scrutiny given to drug prices over the last few years by this and other Congressional Committees, would send a strong message that skyrocketing price increases would no longer be tolerated. Unfortunately, the message is apparently falling on deaf ears within most of the drug manufacturing industry ... prices are increasing this year at a rate that actually exceeds the unprecedented inflation rates of the 1980s." A few years later, President Bill Clinton publicly slammed the drugmakers, and the nation weighed a health-care reform plan that would have established a price-review board for drugs (albeit one with little actual power). The drug industry lobbied hard, then hunkered down, cutting back on spending and watching its stocks decline—only to rebound exuberantly with the junking of the Clinton plan and the go-ahead for TV advertising.

The dawn of the twenty-first century finds the drug industry at a crossroads, under increasing scrutiny, but, in some cases at least, taking greater liberties than ever. Having become ever more expert in such areas as advertising, political lobbying, and brand extension, the industry builds and protects today's best-selling products but risks sacrificing a far more valuable asset: its reputation as above all an "ethical" enterprise allied with the sober ethos of science.

# [conclusion]

TODAY, many Americans, feeling outdone by this sly goose of an industry, are frustrated. And angry. Ohioan Louise Carroll takes twelve prescription drugs. Four generics for blood pressure and depression together average less than $100 a month. But local prices for the others, including Nexium for digestive problems, Lipitor for cholesterol, Vioxx for arthritis, and Zyrtec for allergies, add up to about $570 a month. What gives these drug companies the right to charge so much? And who will help Carroll figure out what she's getting for her money? "The real problem is with the drug companies," she says. "They talk about research and development, but they're advertising all over TV and in all the magazines. Then there are the kudos for doctors and all the free drugs. It's like, 'You grease my palm and I'll grease yours.'"

"I spent forty years as an engineer in the aerospace business and I know what companies who support the Department of Defense get paid," says Eugene Cairns, of New York state. "I know what they get paid in the way of profits, and I know what R&D is. Price controls? When we sold to the government, we competed [for contracts], and if that isn't a price control I'll eat my hat." He takes generics when he can. "When I found out I had a hiatal hernia they had me on Prilosec. After things got under control my doctor said, 'Take Tagamet [available in generic form]—it's a lot cheaper and it'll do the same thing.'" At his last checkup, Cairns was able to reduce the dosage.

"I have to be candid, I can afford the U.S. prices," says Graham Hay, a former New York advertising executive. "But I became familiar with the Canadian prices and I was just so incensed by the difference that I proceeded to find out more about it, and it just made me madder and madder." Hay thinks the answer is to shorten the patent life for brand drugs. "The pharmaceutical companies are saying they're coming up with plans for discounts to Medicare patients— that's fine, but what about the rest of the people in this country? Are they chopped liver? Don't they get a 20-percent discount, too?"

In response to the public mood, government, too, is drawing a bead on the industry. The FTC, Department of Justice, and state attorneys general are all probing either the drugmakers' marketing or pricing practices, or both. State governments are moving aggressively to contain prices. And though 2002 midterm election victories for drugmakers' Republican allies made substantive congressional action a dim possibility, representatives on both sides of the aisle are taking pains to, at the very least, not appear like drug-company shills. In all, it's not hard to see why Sager calls drug-industry execs "the most nervous very well-dressed people around." Or as one government prosecutor puts it, "They're getting spanked."

What's the industry going to do about it? A number of companies have relieved some of the pressure by establishing discount cards for low-income seniors, or, for example, lowering the price of AIDS drugs in Africa. A couple of top executives have made it clear they don't think it's good business to game the system with patent-extension high jinks. Some industry supporters see its problem as a public-relations failure and criticize the trade group PhRMA for clinging to we're-going-to-save-your-life rhetoric instead of making real arguments about international pricing, the value of pharmaceuticals, and the fine points of R&D. Others see the predicament in broader terms. Ehrlich, believing industry leaders can benefit from listening to outside perspectives, has invited to Rx Insight's 2003 conference for marketing people none other than staunch critic Ralph Nader. "The pharmaceutical industry is now the most resented industry," another marketing executive said at the roundtable printed in *Pharmaceutical Executive*. "And that probably is because we're having something of an identity crisis ourselves. What are we really about? Is it about making money? Is it about saving lives? Obviously the answer is yes and yes ... [But it's] not the number of products that defines success or failure; it's the size of the profits. It only takes one Claritin to drive more revenue than you get for 15 orphan drugs ... I'm not talking about public relations; I'm talking about the public. The public resents the concept of us being only money-driven. They want needed products, not just giant products."

Still, the central industry response to public outrage has

been to once again toss out its line about R&D, batten down the hatches, and wait for the skies to clear. Ultimately, of course corporations *are* money driven. As Reinhardt says, "This industry—and I would do it too—would use absolutely every means, every trick that works, every argument, to keep the money flowing into the industry."

The question for us as Americans is whether we will allow public health to be money driven as well. What are *we* really about? What, ultimately, is more offensive to Americans— government regulation or the fact that a new drug for leukemia costs almost $30,000 a year? Authorizing Medicare to negotiate for better prices or forcing taxpayers to write the drug industry a blank check? Which is more problematic for free speech: limiting the drug industry's marketing or letting it buy a "share of voice" so substantial it jams the signals, with Big Pharma playing on every station, all day, in research, in clinical care, in Washington?

Here's what goes on in America: A pregnant Pennsylvania woman just diagnosed with a rare blood disease calls a local Red Cross program for an emergency one-month supply of the $650 drug she needs. She doesn't qualify. "Have you got any family you can talk to?" asks the program coordinator. A pause, then, "Well, I suppose I can ask them." A college student drops out temporarily because he's having seizures, loses insurance coverage as a result, and can't pay for his epilepsy drug. Dolores and Larry Alstodt of Florida wrestle with whether to continue their mortgage or buy medicine; she has acutely painful arthritis and a serious lung condition. And Jon Graham of Ohio, concerned that his medications are depleting the savings that he and his wife, Lela, have accrued, decides to make a three-month supply last six months. His blood pressure and blood sugar shoot up. He's nauseated, lightheaded. He goes back on the regimen. "I thought that when I retired I'd have a roof over my head, a car, and enough money where I'd be able to relax and have a little fun," he says ruefully. "But instead it's buy medicines and stay in the house all the time."

In the 2000 Kaiser Family Foundation–*NewsHour* survey, nearly three out of ten Americans said they'd failed to fill a prescription because it cost too much. Meanwhile, untold numbers of people (or their insurers) are paying top dollar for a once-a-day version of a drug they could get at a fraction of the cost in a twice-a-day generic. They're snapping up expensive new drugs as soon as the samples are dropped rather than waiting to see whether the drug really fits their condition or whether it's truly better than cheaper, older drugs. As consumers, as workers, as taxpayers, Americans have subsidized the growth of the global pharmaceutical industry, with virtually no strings attached. Sure, we want the new medicines. But are we really to believe that growing the pharmaceuticals business is synonymous with "growing" the health of our children and elderly? Don't we, as keepers of the industry, even get to ask that question?

It is not beyond the imagination or the wealth of Americans to design a method for getting the right medicines to people who need them at a reasonable price. A first and necessary step would be for our leaders to accept that they can not promote the well-being of ordinary Americans while everywhere accommodating the demands of the drug industry and other commercial interests. "We have a choice among suffering and dying for lack of needed drugs, paying more and more for drugs, or reform," says Sager. "We can stop torturing ourselves. Reform is obviously the only humane choice."

There's been a contradiction in how we think about the cost of drugs. On the one hand, the American reverence for a free market makes us reluctant to regulate the business of drugmaking. On the other hand, we grant the industry various lucrative advantages in that market—from secrecy in pricing to tax breaks to extraordinary access for its salespeople—on the grounds that it is special somehow, not just a business. It's almost as if the insistent blindness of American institutions, perhaps even of the public itself, has given the drug industry little choice but to make its preposterous claims. My, what a big advertising budget you have! All the better to educate you, my dears. My, what a team of lobbyists you have! All the better to protect the search for tomorrow's cures, my dears. Drugs produce social good, but they are also a business, a big business, and one that, for a long time, has been making the rules by which it operates. Like the childhood bully on the block, increasingly unpopular but seemingly invincible, maybe the drugmakers are really asking a desperate question: *Who's going to stop me?*

## [sources and acknowledgments]

THIS BOOK began when Denise Mitchell, public affairs director of the AFL-CIO, called me with an idea: She wanted a clear-sighted, accessible piece of writing on how the prescription drugs business works in America. After I finished the piece in the summer of 2002, she showed it to Donna Jablonski, the AFL-CIO's deputy director of public affairs, who believed enough in the project to suggest it should be published as a book. Having sponsored the work but otherwise left me entirely to my own devices, the AFL-CIO now passed it along to Peter Osnos at PublicAffairs, who invited me to expand the manuscript and undertook to publish it on an accelerated schedule. David Patterson, my editor at PublicAffairs, amiably and very ably shepherded the book to its final stages.

I am fortunate indeed that my work fell into the hands of these four creative individuals and received their generous support. Although as a practical matter the reporting wasn't different from work I'd done for newspapers or magazines, its spirit was informed by the traditions of the union movement and of independent publishing.

I thank the people who spoke to me about their own lives: families struggling with chronic illness and unmanageable drug bills, an Iowa nurse, the rural drug rep, the local pharmacist, to name a few. Their concrete experiences focused my thinking and sharpened my sense of purpose. I am also grateful to Art Hilgart, whose many years in the drug industry led him to a critique of its current practices that is insistent but hardly bitter; I learned a great deal during the hours we spent talking about, among other topics, the fascinating history of the business. Numerous scholars were generous with their time. I am especially indebted to Alan Sager of the Boston University School of Public Health and Steven Findlay of the National Institute for Health Care Management for reading the manuscript and offering their intelligent and informed responses.

As readers will have recognized, this book draws on the work of many others. I have erred on the side of naming sources within the text. For good measure, let me name them here, too. The advocacy groups Public Citizen, Families USA, the Center for Responsive Politics, the AARP, the Consumer Project on Technology, the National Women's Health Network, and the Center for Policy Alternatives have all conducted invaluable primary research into various aspects of this story. So have several policy-research organizations, most notably the National Institute for Health Care Management and the Henry J. Kaiser Family Foundation. I gained much from following excellent reporting in the *Wall Street Journal* and the *New York Times*, as well as research and commentary in the *New England Journal of Medicine*, the *Journal of the American Medical Association*, the *British Medical Journal*, and *Health Affairs*.

Thanks to my first readers, David Andrews, Linda Greider, and William Greider; to my last reader, the skilled copy editor Michele Wynn; and to any reader who may wish to follow.

[ index ]

PublicAffairs is a publishing house founded in 1997. It is a tribute to the standards, values, and flair of three persons who have served as mentors to countless reporters, writers, editors, and book people of all kinds, including me.

I. F. STONE, proprietor of *I. F. Stone's Weekly*, combined a commitment to the First Amendment with entrepreneurial zeal and reporting skill and became one of the great independent journalists in American history. At the age of eighty, Izzy published *The Trial of Socrates,* which was a national bestseller. He wrote the book after he taught himself ancient Greek.

BENJAMIN C. BRADLEE was for nearly thirty years the charismatic editorial leader of *The Washington Post.* It was Ben who gave the *Post* the range and courage to pursue such historic issues as Watergate. He supported his reporters with a tenacity that made them fearless and it is no accident that so many became authors of influential, best-selling books.

ROBERT L. BERNSTEIN, the chief executive of Random House for more than a quarter century, guided one of the nation's premier publishing houses. Bob was personally responsible for many books of political dissent and argument that challenged tyranny around the globe. He is also the founder and longtime chair of Human Rights Watch, one of the most respected human rights organizations in the world.

For fifty years, the banner of Public Affairs Press was carried by its owner Morris B. Schnapper, who published Gandhi, Nasser, Toynbee, Truman, and about 1,500 other authors. In 1983, Schnapper was described by *The Washington Post* as "a redoubtable gadfly." His legacy will endure in the books to come.

Peter Osnos, *Publisher*